THE SERPENT WITHIN

Politics, Literature and American Individualism

JOSEPH C. BERTOLINI

University Press of America, Inc.
Lanham · New York · Oxford

Copyright © 1997 by
University Press of America,® Inc.
4720 Boston Way
Lanham, Maryland 20706

12 Hid's Copse Rd.
Cummor Hill, Oxford OX2 9JJ

All rights reserved
Printed in the United States of America
British Library Cataloguing in Publication Information Available

Library of Congress Cataloging-in-Publication Data

Bertolini, Joseph
The serpent within : politics, literature and American individualism /
Joseph C. Bertolini.
p. cm.
1. Individualism--United States. 2. Social integration--United States.
3. Literature and society--United States. 4. American literature--
History and criticism. I. Title.
HM136B43 1996   302.5'4'0973--dc21   96-40871 CIP

ISBN 0-7618-0626-1 (pbk: alk. ppr.)

The paper used in this publication meets the minimum
requirements of American National Standard for information
Sciences—Permanence of Paper for Printed Library Materials,
ANSI Z39.48—1984

To Martha,
best friend, wife, helpmate
and best antidote to the 4 A.M. scaries

Contents

Acknowledgments	vii
Chapter 1 Introduction: The Serpent Within	1
Chapter 2 Hobbes and Locke in America	13
Chapter 3 *The Scarlet Letter*	31
Chapter 4 *Moby-Dick*	51
Chapter 5 *Huckleberry Finn*	65
Chapter 6 *The Great Gatsby*	79
Chapter 7 Literature, Individualism and Public Policy	89
Index	113

Acknowledgments

Due to the complexity of my professional life, this book took a couple of years to complete. During the entire time, my wife, Martha, provided constant support and technical advice. She retyped the entire manuscript and made constant and valued editorial suggestions. Without her assistance, given my schedule, this book probably could not have been written.

The work of H. Mark Roelofs, my mentor and now colleague at New York University, has had a significant germinative effect on portions of my thesis. Above all, I thank him for his inspiring, passionate commitment to the power and importance of ideas.

I also wish to thank my friend of forty-five years, Paul Many, of the University of Toledo, for his creative ideas with regard to the *Huckleberry Finn* chapter and for his unswerving and warm support for all my writing projects during my years in the wilderness. Additionally, I am grateful to Bill Nester, my St. John's colleague, for reading several of the chapters, making perceptive comments and also providing invaluable encouragement and support.

I am also thankful for the kind encouragement and helpful technical suggestions provided by Michelle Harris and Helen Hudson of University Press and by Dorothy Albritton of Majestic Wordsmith.

Of course, my students over the years have been a constant inspiration. They have helped me, in our discussions, both in and out of class, to clarify and develop my ideas. I am grateful for all the time I have spent with them.

But, in the end, an author always has to acknowledge his own final responsibility for what has been produced. Thus, I alone am responsible for anything the reader wishes to criticize.

Chapter 1

Introduction: The Serpent Within

In 1843, Nathaniel Hawthorne wrote a particularly penetrating short story entitled "Egotism, or the Bosom Serpent." The tale was about Roderick Elliston, who believed he had a gnawing serpent living inside him. It wasn't *really* supposed to be there, of course. Rather, the snake in the man's bosom was supposed to be the symbol of a monstrous egotism to which everything was referred[1] — and he was not the only one in this condition. According to "Roderick's theory, every mortal bosom harbored"[2] such a monster. He believed that "there is poisonous stuff in any man's heart sufficient to generate a brood of serpents."[3] And it seemed to be a problem from which the individual could not escape. "Could I for one instant forget myself," Roderick said, "The serpent might not abide within me. It is my diseased self-contemplation that has engendered and nourished him."[4]

In his condition, Roderick had no concern for others or for the larger society. In fact, he took sadistic satisfaction in mocking and taunting others whom he knew also harbored serpents. Thus he was consumed with himself, engaging in excessive, egoistic individualism, cut off from the larger community, inflicting suffering on others and pathologically unhappy.

In the end, he is saved, at least temporarily, by the forgiving love of a woman whom he had earlier abandoned. So the story ends on a hopeful note, but Hawthorne was too wise to be a simple optimist — or a simple pessimist either, for that matter. Roderick does have a genuine, albeit brief, transcendent moment at the end of the tale, but we are left to wonder if his improved condition will persist. It may, of course, but given the case Hawthorne made in the story, and what we know of the author's philosophy, the greater likelihood is that it will not.

Roderick had asked, in the allegory, to be able to forget himself for one instant and this he had achieved at the end. But he had also attributed his problem to "diseased self-contemplation," a condition for which there would be no easy relief — especially in America. Chances are that the problem would arise again for Roderick, particularly since he dwelled within an American culture that would foster "diseased self-contemplation," or, to use more reserved terminology, excessive, egoistic individualism.

Further, this American problem has become worse with time. Since Hawthorne's day we have become more individualistic than ever. Egotism, the concern with self that leads to a disconnection with others, has only intensified in America as our history has unfolded. And there is no ready antidote. "Hawthorne turned to American history, the history of alienation" to try to find some way of overcoming this atomism, which was readily apparent to him by the mid-19th century, and found that all that "isolatoes had in common, their magnetic chain, was precisely the spiritual history of their isolation."[5] Nonetheless, in his work, Hawthorne continued to search for relief from his American condition. He sought, in effect, "the center of a world where centers do not hold."[6] He would relate it fleetingly here and there — the ending of "Egotism," for example, or the chapter, "A Flood of Sunshine," in *The Scarlet Letter*, but he always returned to his dark, critical analysis of American culture.

*****

My thesis is that there is a gnawing serpent existing inside the American civic body that seems to be slowly devouring it. This serpent is our excessive, atomistic individualism. The problem is rooted in our Hobbesian-Lockean socio-political culture and it is intensifying with time. With our individualism becoming more and more extreme,

Introduction: The Serpent Within 3

we are less and less able even to articulate any viable conception of community. We can speak coherently of rights, but not of responsibilities.[7] The idea of Self is meaningful to us, but the reality of Other becomes less and less comprehensible. Any ideas of community extant today are essentially the residue of the social and moral capital of earlier generations.

By the middle of the last century, the most insightful literary people of the time could see where we were going. Of course, any list of great literary minds of the 19th century would have to include Nathaniel Hawthorne, Herman Melville and Mark Twain. A case can be made for each of them having written "the great American novel." And any list of perceptive early 20th century writers would have to include F. Scott Fitzgerald, if only because of his one really outstanding book, *The Great Gatsby*.

I argue that these writers are great American authors precisely because they perceive, describe and inform us about the nature and consequences of that which most makes us uniquely American — our individualism. They could see its virtues and they understood its danger. They knew that the Self in America had a way of expanding out of all proportion to any workable relationship to community. They realized that both our salvation and our damnation were wrapped up with the idea of individualism and that, ironically, the very quality that was the source of the nation's greatness, the concept of autonomous selfhood, could also be the cause of its destruction.

Understanding individualism, then, as it is practiced in America, became, for them, a subject of inquiry, concern and prescription. Knowing where we were and where we were going, they had ideas about what we should and should not do. Their prescience allowed them to comprehend the consequences of individualism for us today.

Of course, choosing four particular authors to focus upon always requires an explanation of one's grounds for selection. I am certainly not arguing that the group of novelists selected for inquiry here constitutes an exclusive "great writers" list. One could obviously make the case for including Henry James or William Faulkner or Ernest Hemingway, for example, in any such basic collection. Each of them would clearly be a classic American writer and each addressed the nature of the American individual and his relationship to the larger community. Further, a case for inclusion could be made for a number of contemporary American writers including John Updike, William Styron, Saul Bellow, J.D.Salinger or John Irving.

The list of the excluded could go on and on, but any such study as this requires selection and, inevitably, omission. Exclusion naturally results when one focuses on a particular time period. I chose to focus primarily on the fertile mid-19th century when the real nature of individualist American culture was first becoming evident to our most sensitive literary analysts. As we developed our own unique culture, when we realized that our literature was not European literature *manqué,* the nature of the American soul became stunningly evident.

Certainly, Hawthorne, Melville, Twain and Fitzgerald were masterful at cutting through so much of the superficiality of the everyday concerns of their time to see what really lay at the heart of our struggles. They could see that our basic problem was not just a matter of north and south or rich and poor or capital and labor, but something much deeper. Indeed, these questions took on a different meaning when the American context was properly understood. For them, America was the land in which primary focus was on the highly individualized Self — that was a given. But could we still then relate to Other? Could the nation endure as any kind of whole if we were all to be perpetually ensconced in our own little worlds?

The four writers primarily addressed here all suggest, in one form or another, and, of course, indirectly, that we can only survive with an enriched, less materialistic, more enlightened form of individualism. They knew that we could never abandon our individualism or replace it with anything else, that it is our nature to be what we are but, perhaps, by returning to our relatively more pristine, less self-centered and more other-regarding, Jeffersonian origins we could avoid the danger of atomistic alienation (Twain). Or perhaps we could appreciate the value of the Western tragic tradition. The starkness of our aloneness could compel us to appreciate the primal nature of the Self-Other question. The tragic self, rich in complexity, could find profound possibility in a country in which the individual can never be one with others (Hawthorne). Or, in a variation of this, perhaps the Self could appreciate its aloneness in the universe and reach to the world beyond its epithelial boundaries with openness, with a desire to appreciate others in their existential aloneness. When we fully realize we are each up against All, we accept this situation, impose no ideology on it and try to imagine what it must be for others to be in the same existential condition that faces oneself (Melville).

And if the growing awareness of the distinct nature of American culture in the 19th century compelled Hawthorne, Melville and Twain

Introduction: The Serpent Within 5

to understand the American mind so nakedly revealed to them, then one might suspect that the catastrophic effect of the First World War on the Western mind and, in particular, the American mind, would have a somewhat similar, jarring effect. The American writers of the "lost generation," of which Fitzgerald is certainly one of the most prominent, were faced with a Western culture that had seemingly destroyed all of its sustaining myths. And since they knew the American version of this culture best, they turned on it with a vengeance, searching out its roots and revealing its flaws. They wrote as if America had been fooled for so many years prior to the war, as if the lessons of Melville, Hawthorne and Twain had been lost in the evident material success of industrialization, urbanization and commercialism. They went right at the heart of what they saw as America's flaw — a shallow, materialist, excessive individualism.[8]

Of all these later, post World War I novelists, however, Fitzgerald provided the most acute analysis in *The Great Gatsby*. In a clean, spare parable he told the tale of an American individualism that had been corrupted by vulgar materialism and was self-destructing, although it still possessed remnants of that more decent, idealized individualism of our past. Gatsby believed that the purpose of the individual's quest was love, love of another self. For our Puritan ancestors, the purpose of Protestant, Puritan individualism was the love of God. In both cases, there was a goal beyond acquisitiveness, beyond immediate self-interest. Material wealth, for the Puritans, was a sign of God's favor — it was the road to salvation. It was seen as a sign of God's love. For Gatsby, materialism was the way to get Daisy to love him, but Daisy was too superficial to appreciate Gatsby's profound dimension. He wanted transcendent, spiritually intense love, but she wanted things. She wept over his collection of shirts, for example. The destructive conclusion of the novel is what happens, Fitzgerald suggests, when the American idea of individualism becomes merely self-referential, without even a viable conception of anything beyond itself. Daisy just had no idea of what Gatsby was trying to do, of how potentially profound he really was. Like most Americans, Fitzgerald implies, Daisy was out of her league with anyone who possessed real individualist depth. Gatsby's Other-regardedness was already rare by the 1920's, incomprehensible to others (except Nick) and doomed.

In a way, all four authors have written pointed jeremiads warning about what we will become if we do not, then, develop our individualism in a different, more profound, more creative form. All four wrote at moments in our history when our real nature was becoming most clearly revealed to us. After them, one could argue, fine American writing is all extrapolation on that same theme of the isolated self who must acquire some depth or perish.

But, additionally, *The Scarlet Letter, Moby-Dick, Huckleberry Finn* and *The Great Gatsby* have been selected for analysis because there is a general, considerable consensus as to their being "great works." By utilizing such a consensual sample, I decrease the risk of choosing authors that are not truly representative of the depths of the American individualist mind-set.

My choice further rests on an arbitrary decision to confine this project to novels written prior to the second World War. I would venture to suggest, however, that the choice of virtually any other significant writer in our history would confirm my thesis that American novelists exemplify Hobbesian-Lockean liberal culture. It is just that the writers that I selected for the above reasons do this better and with greater insight and with more lessons for us than most others probably would.

Actually, it should not really come as a surprise that these authors reveal to us the nature of the American culture. After all, they are Americans, and brilliant ones at that. Having grown up in our culture, they absorbed it and then wrote about it, uncovering a cultural essence that most Americans would be too much a part of to see clearly. If individualism, or more properly, Hobbesian-Lockean liberalism, is at the heart of American thinking, most people would just take it for granted or see it as common sense, for it would affect every sphere of American life. Family, religion, economics, politics and literature, of course, would all be expressive of the same *weltanschauung*. Studies of political culture, for example, make clear that political ideas and political behavior are always rooted in a given cultural matrix, that culture significantly influences behavior.[9] Politics and literature, then, would necessarily have the same ideological foundation. Hence, in a given culture, political and literary ideas, at their core, should be basically similar. Politics and literature should be, ultimately, about the same cultural concerns. Further, we should be able to turn to either politics or literature to help us better understand the other, particularly if both are simply different expressions of the same values.

It is an additional presumption of this study that we can employ the insights offered to us in our most insightful American literature to better comprehend our political situation in America and, indeed, to

Introduction: The Serpent Within 7

gain perspective on how to address, in a very general sense, political problems. In our contemporary politics, we can often lose sight of that which we all hold in common, for example. We can exaggerate differences that really, at essence, are culturally trivial. On the other hand, we might assume that we have come together to solve an issue, that we have formulated a community response when, in fact, we have only reconfigured our Hobbesian-Lockean individualist collision along new lines. Our great writers should be able to get our analysis back on track, to get us to focus on the essence of how we think and behave. Only by fully comprehending our ideational foundation can we understand the socio-political edifice we have built upon it and the problems ingrained in that structure today.

In fact, within the discipline of political science, there is an expanding awareness of the importance of literature in the understanding of politics for precisely these reasons. In earlier decades, there was a great emphasis on the study of politics as a social science. Facts about politics were accumulated and quantifiable data was amassed. The focus was on observable patterns of political behavior,[10] but this behavioralist approach often failed to address the unique aspects of political events and to focus sufficiently on the importance of ideas and cultural values in determining political conduct. The resulting post-behavioralist revolution led the discipline to be "more pluralistic in its definition of subject matter" and even to "look to works of art for enlightenment" concerning "the aspects of human life that are most difficult, if not impossible, to study and observe externally or objectively — the attitudes, emotions, and opinions that shape and are shaped by people's circumstances, especially their political circumstances."[11] In fact, the argument was made that it is in the political study of literature that we can gain critical insight into political culture, since literature is really " an expression of the popular culture that has such a pervasive, if amorphous, effect on political life."[12]

Besides the linkage between political culture and literature, this study is also predicated on an essential nexus between literature and philosophy and, specifically, in this case, political philosophy. After all, "they indubitably cover the same ground. They both specialize in the great and greatest themes."[13] Actually, it should be rather presumed that political ideas and literary themes *should* coincide in a given culture, at least in their larger aspects, otherwise a culture, or, at least, that part of it, would not be coherent and would be awash in cognitive dissonance. So these novels have been approached "as forms of American political thought. . . . Understanding the novels in this way both enriches our sense of them as *oeuvres* and — at the same time — enriches our understanding of the political philosophy on which the American regime rather explicitly rests."[14]

If one is searching, thus, for the principal motivating impulses at the root of a given people's political culture, it would seem that one must also study that people's political philosophy and literature since they are all derived from the same basic, cultural foundation. In the next chapter, I will present the argument that American socio-political culture is essentially Hobbesian-Lockean and that, consequently, its primary literature is immersed in Hobbesian-Lockean ideas. The four novelists to be discussed in later chapters, I attest, were at least intuitively aware of the nature of these ideas, in both their positive and negative aspects, and saw this cognitive matrix, again consciously or not, as *the* matter to address since they knew it lay at the root of everything important that happened in American society. They were so finely aware, so viscerally cognizant, of the nation's heartbeat that they did not have to possess a conscious working knowledge of the structure of Hobbesian-Lockean thought. They would not have had to have read either Hobbes or Locke to experience that we are Hobbesian-Lockean to our roots. If, as I shall argue, Louis Hartz, in particular, is correct about the nature of the American political psyche, all one has to do is spend any length of time in American society and one absorbs classic liberal thinking as if by osmosis. A sensitive visitor like Tocqueville or highly sensitive residents like Hawthorne, Melville, Twain and Fitzgerald would automatically incorporate our cultural perspective into the marrow of their bones and be able to address it with authority. This, in fact, is what they did.

In addition, I would point out how *not* to think of this project. It is, first of all, not primarily a work of literary criticism. If one must stress priorities, then I must make it clear that I am utilizing American literature primarily to support a given interpretation of American political culture. I am interested primarily in using this literature to reinforce the argument that we are all Hobbesian-Lockean at heart and then to demonstrate how these brilliantly incisive authors saw the dark side of this situation and composed an overall perspective on how we should cope with it. As I will argue in the last chapter, Melville and the others came to a remarkable agreement on what we were about, where we had gone wrong and how, in rough design, we should deal with our flawed condition, with the serpent in the Edenic garden, so to speak. They all identified American individualism as

Introduction: The Serpent Within 9

both positive and negative, so they knew us well. But, again, I approach these writers as a political philosopher, not as a literary critic, with all attendant apologies to specialists of the latter category.

Also, this should not be construed as a study of expressly *political* novels. I am not arguing that any of the four works discussed in this book are *primarily* about politics. Irving Howe defined a political novel as one in which "political ideas play a dominant role or in which the political milieu is the dominant setting."[15] In this sense, *none* of the four novels I have chosen are *political* novels. None of them are mainly about politics, *per se*. By the term *political* novel, Howe had in mind such works as Henry Adam's *Democracy*, Dostoevsky's *The Possessed*, Conrad's *The Secret Agent*, Orwell's *1984*, Solzhenitsyn's *The First Circle* or Joe Klein's *Primary Colors*. All of them are specifically about politics. *Huckleberry Finn*, on the other hand, I argue, is about a particular *weltanschauung*, an individualist mindset, that is reflective of a culture that gives rise both to American literature and to American politics. It is not a *political novel*, but a novel that addresses the same set of ideas that lies at the base of *our* political tradition. By understanding Twain's novel we understand our politics better, but *Huckleberry Finn* is not specifically a political work.

Further, while I have made some references to other works by the four authors, I have essentially confined this study to the specific works referred to above. Given the limits of any such inquiry, it would not be feasible to address all the works of these writers. While it can be generally assumed that a similar attitude toward individualism is to be found in their other works, my argument rests on the four selected books, not on the authors' overall output. Including Melville's *Pierre*, Hawthorne's *The Blithedale Romance*, Twain's *The Mysterious Stranger* and Fitzgerald's *The Last Tycoon* would have made this project too unwieldy. They will have to wait for another time.

Finally, as aforementioned, an underlying purpose of this project is to defend the thesis that American socio-political culture is primarily Lockean liberal. This argument, most clearly expostulated by Louis Hartz, is regarded as the standard interpretation of the American mind, but it is often under attack, particularly now by the civic republican argument and the communitarian critique.[16] By demonstrating that these four great works of American literature are all supportive of the Lockean thesis (and its Hobbesian underpinnings), I would hope to further strengthen the latter critique against its opponents.

If, however, the Hobbesian-Lockean liberal thesis is correct, then there are serious implications for American politics. But these implications were essentially, largely intuitively, foreseen and given literary shape by Hawthorne, Melville, Twain and Fitzgerald. By examining their complex works, we can gain understanding as to how they believed we should deal with our greatest cultural problem, the danger of unbridled, superficial individualism — the serpent within.

Notes

1. Nathaniel Hawthorne, "Egotism, or, the Bosom Serpent," in *The Celestial Railroad and Other Stories* (New York: New American Library, 1963), 176.
2. Ibid., 179.
3. Ibid., 183.
4. Ibid., 183.
5. Charles Feidelson, Jr., "The Scarlet Letter," in *Hawthorne Centenary Essays,* ed. Roy Harvey Pearce (Columbus, Ohio: Ohio State University Press, 1964), 32.
6. Ibid., 34.
7. See e.g. Amitai Etzioni, *The Spirit of Community* (New York: Simon and Schuster, 1993).
8. See Sherwood Anderson, *Winesburg, Ohio* (New York: Viking, 1958) and Sinclair Lewis, *Main Street* (New York: Harcourt, Brace, 1920).
9. For classics dealing with political culture see e.g. Gabriel Almond and Sidney Verba, eds., *The Civic Culture* (Boston: Little, Brown, 1963) and *The Civic Culture Revisited* (Boston: Little, Brown, 1980) and Lucian Pye and Sidney Verba, eds., *Political Culture and Political Development* (Princeton: Princeton University Press, 1965).
10. See David Easton, *A Systems Analysis of Political Life* (New York: Wiley, 1965).
11. Catherine Zuckert, "Why Political Scientists Want to Study Literature," *Political Science and Politics* 28, no. 2 (June, 1995): 189.
12. Ibid., 189.
13. Werner J. Dannhauser, "Poetry vs. Philosophy," *Political Science and Politics* 28, No. 2 (June, 1995): 191.
14. Catherine Zuckert, *Natural Right and the American Imagination: Political Philosophy in Novel Form* (Savage, Maryland: Rowman and Littlefield, 1990), ix.
15. Irving Howe, *Politics and the Novel* (New York: Columbia University Press, 1957), 17.
16. Both perspectives are discussed in Chapter 2.

Chapter 2
Hobbes and Locke in America

I

Louis Hartz, in his seminal and highly regarded work, *The Liberal Tradition in America,* argued that American society "begins with Locke and . . . stays with Locke, by virtue of an absolute and irrational attachment it develops for him."[1] Americans, he held, were Lockean liberals through and through. He used the term "liberal" in its classic, Lockean, pre-twentieth century understanding of the term to refer to an autonomous individual born with rights that government must protect. This liberal interpretation of American sociopolitical culture is generally regarded as the consensual point of view.[2]

Locke argues that the individual is the essential locus of value, that all individuals are born with rights and that the state exists to protect these rights. Originally, he speculates, people existed essentially autonomously in a "state of nature," but then joined together to establish government when it became clear that life and property were insecure without the protection of political authority. He believes that there would always be some people who would attempt to harm you and seize your property if not for fear of the state's policing power.[3]

Lockean thought became dominant in England, particularly after the Glorious Revolution of 1688, but it always had to contend with a continuing feudal tradition and with radicalism, feudalism's evolving counterpart. Also, Locke, being a gentleman and a 17th century man, assumes that even if every man is an autonomous entity, he nonetheless exists in a web of social interrelationships that, in effect, act to restrain self-interest. He assumes a British, a European, sense of community that would naturally tend to bind separated selves together.

In America, the Lockean individualist idea became unbridled. Entering at Plymouth and Jamestown and continuing through the birth of the new nation, the Lockean idea of each man being an autonomous self who is entitled to that with which he combines his labor became palpable reality. The great, expansive continent, awash with natural wealth,[4] made it theoretically and, in many cases, practically possible to become a success "on your own hook," as New England fishermen would say. Hard work and self-reliance seemed to be all one needed. Further, there was no oppressive feudal order, no ingrained class structure to contend with and no corresponding peasant solidarity to make bourgeois individualism seem similarly repressive. Government was minimal and oriented toward *laissez-faire*. It seemed as if the philosophy of individualism was the obvious way to organize a sociopolitical order. Individualism was viewed simply as common sense.

But Locke has dark underpinnings. A strong argument has been made by Roelofs, Macpherson, Coleman, Hofstadter, Strauss and others[5] that Locke is really a diluted variant of Thomas Hobbes. It was, after all, Hobbes, writing prior to Locke and in direct response to the chaos of the English Civil War, who first clearly postulated that each man is an autonomous self, as *ens completum*, born with rights in the state of nature and entirely concerned with his/her own self-interest. Hobbes described life in the state of nature, prior to the existence of government, as a "war of all against all,"[6] resulting in such terrible conditions that life becomes "nasty, brutish and short."[7] All men, then, are like Ishmael, Abraham's son, who is described in Genesis as having "his hand against every man" and who has "every man's hand against him."[8]

Since every person can only understand his own self-interest, Hobbes argues, there is really no alternative to this perpetual conflict.

It is natural and normal for this interpersonal struggle to go on. Even after government has been created to impose order, the struggle continues. It is just not so brutal — at least as long as the government effectively does its job. Murder as a method of getting your way is ostensibly ruled out, but economic and social competition, material aggrandizement at the other's expense and general interpersonal one-upsmanship are not. Each lives in an isolated world without genuine community. There could be no real community because social life is atomized. Each lives in his discrete imagination, wanting all for himself/herself. Since there is no limit to the imagination, but there is a limit as to what one could acquire, since there is always a scarcity of values,[9] men will always be in collision. As Hobbes writes, "If any two men desire the same thing, which nevertheless they cannot both enjoy, they become enemies."[10] The conflict also proceeds on the psychological level, "For every man looketh that his companion should value him, at the same rate he sets upon himself; and upon all signs of contempt, or undervaluing, naturally endeavors, as far as he dares (which amongst them that have no common power to keep them in quiet, is far enough to make them destroy each other), to extort a greater value from his condemners, by damage; and from others, by the example."[11] Thus, "Men have no pleasure, but on the contrary a great deal of grief, in keeping company, where there is no power able to over-awe them all."[12]

Contact with one's fellows, then, is always about rivalry and competition. There is no real empathy. No one can ever understand another. Others are opaque, indecipherable obstacles to the pursuit of one's goals. Conflict and collision, while not always overt, is always present, always implied, always insinuated. "For as the nature of foul weather, lieth not in a shower or two of rain; but in an inclination thereto of many days together: so the nature of war, consisteth not in actual fighting; but in the known disposition thereto, " Hobbes writes.[13] Man's joy, after all, "consisteth in comparing himself with other men"[14] — and the rivalry never ceases, except with death.

Hobbes sees all of this as natural and normal. He is observing man as a scientist would observe nature. This is just the way it is, he argues. To say that people should *not* act and think as Hobbes describes is pointless. They *will* behave this way, he says, and that is all there is to it. What's more, it is their right to act as they wish. "The right of nature . . . is the liberty each man hath to use his own power, as he will himself, for the preservation . . . of his own life; and consequently, of doing any thing, which in his own judgment, and reason, he shall conceive to be the aptest means thereunto."[15] What *you* want to do is good. What blocks you from getting it is bad. "Good and evil are names that signify our appetites and aversions."[16] They have no objective reality. Good is what allows you to maximize your liberty, the definition of which is "the absence of external impediments." [17] Do what you want, get what you want. There is no alternative. Only the strong state prevents total chaos.

Since man is as self-interested as he is and since *every* man is potentially out to get you, Hobbes argues that peace and order could only be guaranteed by some form of dictatorial sovereign. For Locke, writing in defense of the Glorious Revolution, such a drastic solution is unnecessary since only the *occasional* miscreant wants your life or your property. Most people, Locke believes, would leave you alone. Besides, Locke holds, government can become your enemy as well. It could abuse its power, oppress you and deny you your rights. Thus, the only proper form of government will be a democratic government which, presumably, will be strong enough to protect you against your neighbors but not so strong that it could threaten your rights. Democratic control will ensure that the government does what it is supposed to do and no more.[18] Hobbes, though, believes that the sovereign's power could not be limited, democratically or otherwise. To attempt to do so will weaken the state and invite chaos.

In the end, the difference between Hobbes and Locke comes down to a question of degree. Is there really a war of "all against all" or is interpersonal harmony feasible? Can men and women live together in peace, for the most part, as Locke holds, or is perpetual struggle inevitable?

Now, essentially, both Hobbes and Locke ground their work on the same fundamental principles. Both posit a state of nature, an autonomous self as the foundation of all else and the primacy of natural rights. But Hobbes writes in response to the horrors of civil war that he has witnessed while Locke is the apologist for a successful revolution, so they tend to interpret the consequences of their first principles differently. A further point of difference is the fact that Hobbes is also the general founder of the liberal political tradition[19] and therefore views the autonomous self unadorned, i.e. raw. Locke will draw back from this and give a different, gentler spin to Hobbes' ideas by building the assumption of self-restraint into his model. He argued that the individual is motivated by his self-interest alone, but that does not mean the individual will feel he could do *anything*. Very few people in 17th century England felt so unencumbered by societal restraint that they believed they were completely free to do as they wished. Locke naturally assumes that this would always be the case and, given the world around him, one cannot blame him for thinking so. At that time, indeed, people felt restrained by numerous intermediate societal institutions such as family, church, guild, neighborhood and school. They all made demands on the individual that were inculcated and transformed by conscience into self-restraint. Locke is confident that such self-inhibition will persist. Hence, the state's function is to protect the individual's freedom, not to restrain it. Society will do the restraining, a society resting on centuries of history, custom and tradition.

But, as Hobbes had essentially proposed earlier, what if man is seen, in Shakespeare's words, as the "naked, forked animal that he is?"[20] What if the full implications of liberal principles are seen for what they are and for what they imply? What if we sever self from both societal and governmental restraint? Then man is viewed as are all other creatures — totally consumed with self-interest, nakedly selfish. Besides, Hobbes obviously has doubts about the restraining power of intermediate institutions without the overweening presence of governmental power. Only the threat of countervailing force, he believes, could ultimately keep the self in line and only government effectively could and should have this monopoly. If government is weak, family, church and neighborhood could never control the self. Locke bets that these institutions will continue to remain strong and that, therefore, only a limited government will be needed to deal with those few who, so to speak, slip through the interstices of the restraining societal structures.

II

Of course, America was founded when social restraint over the individual was still very powerful, so Locke, and not Hobbes, was the hero of the Founding Fathers. It was presumed that Hobbes was not necessary. Besides, Hobbes advocates dictatorship, which was anathema to men who were fighting to remove the yoke of British tyranny.

But Hobbes was present in Philadelphia anyway. In admitting Locke, the Framers indirectly acknowledged Hobbes too, for both liberal writers had the same premises, differing, as stated above, only in degree. And being good religious, economic and political individualists, they naturally were in general agreement with Calvin and Adam Smith as well. They believed that "a human being was an atom of self-interest,"[21] accepted

> the mercantile image of life as an eternal battleground and assumed the Hobbesian war of all against all; they did not propose to put an end to this war, but merely to stabilize it and make it less murderous. They had no hope and they offered none for any ultimate organic change in the way men conduct themselves. The result was that while they thought self-interest the most dangerous and unbrookable quality of man, they necessarily underwrote it in trying to control it.[22]

The purpose of the Constitution, then, was really to keep the Hobbesian underside of Locke in line. Thus, while the Founding Fathers talked the language of Locke, they knew they were indirectly dealing with man's Hobbesian dimension also.

But they yet assumed that intermediate institutions would foster self-restraint and responsibility. Hence, there was no mention of the latter virtues in the Constitution. The Constitution was all about rights, about limiting government. Government was seen as a potential enemy of the individual and safeguards were erected against its excesses. The new government, they held, could protect us against any potential Hobbesian underside of Lockean America, but it had to be carefully watched. If family, church and neighborhood continued do their job, the worst effects of Hobbesian-Lockean man could be controlled and government could protect us against those that slip through society's grip. At least this was what the Framers presumed.

What they could not envisage was that the idea of individualism, with no real competition in America, would expand beyond what they would surely have considered to be manageable proportions.[23] They had counted on intermediate structures to control the self, but all of the American social institutions that were supposed to perform this function were really products of a European tradition rich in the architecture of religious, social and communal connectives. On this side of the Atlantic, these institutions, without any real orthodox soil to nurture them, gradually faded before the relentless pressure of individualism, particularly after the Civil War, when liberalism firmly and irrevocably linked with capitalism. The "social sense" of Locke and Adam Smith became gradually more associated with sentimentality, while Calvin wedded with industrialism, with Carnegie, and produced the gospel of success.[24]

Tocqueville, by 1835, was perceptively able to see what was coming, pointing out, for example, that the institution of the family in America already, at that time, did not exist in the traditional, European sense. He observed that "As soon as the young American approaches manhood, the ties of filial obedience are relaxed day by day: master of his thoughts, he is soon master of his conduct."[25] Of individualism, in general, he wrote that it "at first only saps the virtues of public life; but, in the long run, it attacks and destroys all others, and is at length absorbed in downright selfishness. Selfishness is a vice as old as the world, which does not belong to one form of society more than to another; individualism is of democratic origin, and it threatens to spread in the same ratio as the equality of condition."[26] In America, with the passage of time, "the number of persons increases" that "acquire the habit of always considering themselves as standing alone, and they are apt to imagine that their own destiny is in their own hands."[27]

But our individualism, as Tocqueville knew, has never been crudely formulaic or simplistic, for we are not just *simple* individualists, constantly becoming more selfish, more extreme in our atomistic autonomy. We are really very *complicated* individualists, with several dimensions to our liberalism. For example, Roelofs posits the thesis that the American liberal conscience is bifurcated into a Bourgeois element and a Protestant element that are "radically united in their celebration of the autonomy of the individual, and, as radically, divided by the absolute irreconcilability of the demands they respectively place on the individual. In consequence, American individualism, the rock on which all else in the American political system is built, is itself, at the core, radically schizophrenic."[28] Religious and bourgeois individualism are in collision, then, because there is "no way the individual American, on being told, on his Protestant side, to pursue love in egalitarian fellowship, could instead pursue a Bourgeois life of self-aggrandizement in adversarial competition with his neighbors without experiencing pain and guilt . . . No matter which way he went, he would be wrong: rapacious if he won, pathetic if he lost."[29]

So, the American mind is split both horizontally and vertically. It is split horizontally in the sense that we believe we are operating in a Lockean world without fully comprehending the Hobbesian dimension below it. Our language of government is Lockean. The conscious emphasis is on Lockean rights and limiting government, but due to the expansion of self and the concomitant decline of our intermediate institutions, the dark, undergirding implications of Hobbes become ever more evident. And the more the self grows, the more we limit government, which, in general liberal theory, is designed to restrict the self. Hence, the progressively more unrestrained self becomes more rapacious, leading to a demand that government become more Hobbesian so as to control a more and more Hobbesian society. But this demand is countered by those who continue to want government to remain limited, fearing that individualism will be gradually squashed by a more repressive state. Yet those who fear their rapacious Hobbesian neighbors specifically want a stronger government to protect their individual rights *vis-a-vis* their immediate fellows. It becomes a matter of whom do you fear the most? Whom do you believe is the greater threat to your freedom — potentially oppressive government or your neighbors, your fellow citizens, who are becoming more and more threatening.

Note that both sides in this debate speak the language of Hobbesian-Lockean liberalism. The consensual ground is liberal individualism. The issue is always how best to protect and expand the self. Even religious conservatives in America want to expand bourgeois capitalist opportunity. And thus we have the second, lateral division, the aforementioned Bourgeois/Protestant complex. Religious conservatives would use the state in Hobbesian fashion to limit what they would consider to be behavior that threatens the fabric of society. But, at the same time, they are for a laissez-faire attitude on the part of government towards the marketplace. So egotism in terms of moral conduct is to be restrained, but it is to be encouraged in terms of capitalist enterprise.[30] Of course, once the genie is out of the bottle, it is difficult to restrict him to one sphere.

On the other hand, advocates of the welfare state and of government regulation of the economy also generally favor a "hands off" governmental approach with regard to personal moral conduct. According to this position, one has a governmentally regulated responsibility to others in the marketplace, but in society, it is a matter of everyone for himself/herself. And, again, this group faces the same problem of not fully appreciating how unbridled individualism in one area affects conduct in other areas.

Hence, conventional "conservative" and "liberal" name tags become meaningless in a debate in which everyone agrees on the principal importance of the autonomous self and everyone agrees that there should be some sense of responsibility towards others, either in society or in the marketplace. But both sides have different chosen foci of responsibility and both sides must inevitably give ground to the expanding Hobbesian ego. Inevitably, also, the Protestant, religious impulse, the one urging us to apply the golden rule in our dealings with others, assumes the form of a rump, nagging conscience. So one can routinely give at the office or contribute to the neediest during the holidays and consider one's social obligation accounted for — at least superficially. Thus, since Calvin entered America when Hobbes did, the former never goes away, but the latter is clearly ascendant. The religious impulse becomes a private way to assuage guilt . We feel better afterwards, then we go back to expanding the Self, materially or socially. This is all a long way from our Puritan founders who clearly subordinated Hobbes to Calvin. It is all in reverse now — and with a vengeance.

Thus, we are caught within the Hobbesian-Lockean, Protestant/ Bourgeois American mind. We are in a double bind in a tight cage and the walls of this box are hard. "To go beyond those limits we would have to seek out alternatives . . . But the American political mind, trapped in the limited vocabularies of its provincialism, does not provide any alternatives to itself."[31] Locke, Calvin and Smith were brought directly to a virgin land in which their ideas had no real opponents among the colonists, for whom individualism will become the only really viable idea. They are still with us and Hobbes, as if he were a mighty subterranean force, has arisen expansively from underneath. Naturally, the philosophies of Aquinas and Rousseau, the ideologies of right and left, have no real credibility here. Advocates of illiberal alternatives tend to get pushed to the lunatic fringe in America.[32] Cultists, communists and Klansmen tend to be more like warped searchers for a communitarian alternative to liberal aloneness. American monolithic liberalism, in the end, brooks no challengers — and the extent to which one is *not* liberal, the extent to which real left or right groups exists, is the extent to which the state and society repress in the name of individualism. Take, for example, the anti-Catholicism of the 19th century, the attempted destruction of the Indian tribes with the Dawes Act, the Red Scare and McCarthyism of the 20's and 50's and the assault on the Waco compound of the Branch Davidians in 1993. After all, the permanent, self-subordinating organic group in America is the natural enemy of the individual. Americans prefer the non-organic, *ad hoc* group, the type that assists alcoholics or lonely hearts or those who want a traffic light erected on a busy corner, i.e. a group designed not to subordinate but, for the moment, to enhance the power of the individual — and then go away.

III

Two final matters must be addressed before concluding this chapter, both involving critiques of the above liberal thesis. My argument, again, is that America was born immersed in classical liberalism and that it remains a classically liberal nation today, despite all the subsequent twists and turns of our political history. The New Deal, for example, following the earlier Progressive era, advocated the idea that government should take more responsibility for combating those factors that negatively impinge on individualism but this was not a substantial deviation from the Hobbesian-Lockean mentality of the Framers. It was merely a modern derivation of primal liberalism, almost a distinction without a difference. If, in fact, the language of modern liberals might seem more oriented to community than that of their forbears, their philosophical underpinnings, their goals, are the same. All liberals, left and right, want maximal freedom for the individual. Some believe that government interference with capitalism is a hindrance in this regard (American conservatives) and others believe that a strong welfare state is indispensable in achieving freedom (modern liberals). But, at root, they only disagree over methods. Their goal, expansive self-autonomy, is the same. This is not to say that conservatives do not possess some illiberal ideas, but only that to the extent that they possess them, they are experiencing cognitive dissonance.

In this light, it is not helpful to attempt to distinguish between "new liberals" and "classical liberals," at least in America. In Europe, one could argue that liberalism, in the twentieth century, should be more properly called social democracy or liberalism with a communitarian impulse.[33] In Europe, liberalism could borrow communitarian elements from strong traditions of orthodoxy and radicalism and weave them into a new, credible synthesis appropriate to the European context. But in America, all devolves back to the Hobbesian center. In America, liberalism has no competing, compelling traditions to borrow from. Liberalism could only *sound* communitarian, at least sometimes, but it could never really *be* communitarian. If, in the 1930's and the 1960's, liberals often flirted with community, the relationship was never, in the end, consummated. Talk of radicalism and of social responsibility, thus, cannot compensate for our Hobbesian-Lockean cultural DNA. With individualism woven into the sinews of our ideological musculature, it was inevitable that 1930's and 1960's radical talk would be absorbed into the suburban 1950's, the me-centered 1970's and the yuppified 1980's. In America, the communitarian temptation is, in the end, another dimension of that nagging Protestant conscience. We insist strenuously that we can't *just* be Hobbesian materialists — *surely* we must be more. The contemporary communitarian vogue has thus become a secular version of our lingering Protestant guilt. Calvin, after all, was with us at the beginning, and he just won't go away. We have always needed him so that we could believe that Hobbes could be managed.

In an interesting, recent case for the idea that communitarian principles can be found in modern liberalism, Will Kymlicka acknowledges that the "developments initiated by the 'new' liberals are really an abandonment of what was definitive of classical liberalism. He says that "Since they reject the principle of 'self-ownership' which characterized one form of classical liberalism (e.g. in Locke), these new liberals should, for some purposes, be called 'social democrats.'"[34]

My argument, in this regard, though, contrary to Kymlicka, is that the taut thread between classical and contemporary liberals cannot be so easily severed, at least in America, where community-oriented political traditions do not have sufficient historical, cultural weight to influence classical liberalism. In America, on the contrary, classical liberalism has intensified and communitarianism is not a viable option but more of a forlorn hope for something other than a progressively more Hobbesian society. In a way, the communitarian impulse is indicative of the wish to return to a less Hobbesian, more Lockean society i.e. one that was *less* rapacious and where there was *more* of a sense of social responsibility. It is a wish to return to an earlier America, when intermediate institutions had a limiting effect on the liberal ego. In America, the communitarian argument is finally nostalgic, while in Europe, Kymlicka's principal focus, it has real viability.[35]

The second critique of the expanded Hartzian thesis [36] which must be addressed is the argument that the liberal tradition is only one of several equally competing traditions of discourse in America. This is a way of arguing that the American intellectual field is much more fertile than Hartz, Macpherson, Roelofs and Diggins would aver. It implies that there are other ways of organizing the Self-Other relationship in America than the convention of liberal individualism and that these other traditions could be tapped for public policy purposes.

The problem with these arguments is that they either tend to exaggerate the significance of a particular interpretation of a line of thought[37] or they tend to create distinctions without an underlying difference.[38] With regard to the former, for example, Pocock's position that the nation was established by the Framers on a foundation of republican, civic virtue and not on liberal self-interest is, of course, partially true, but as Diggins argues, this republican perspective was always in competition with liberalism and, in the end, was essentially swallowed up by it.[39]

Similarly, Abbot's argument for there being "three major 'languages' or traditions of discourse" in America and Smith's "multiple traditions" thesis do not so much refute Hartz as make him more multi-dimensional. They seem to conclude by suggesting that liberalism has more complex variations that would at first appear to be the case and that there are several intellectual substrands in the American mix. Abbot suggests that there are traditions of biblical thought and of civic republicanism in the American culture as well as conservative and radical languages. But he is quick to point out that these non-liberal strains all have "common moorings" with liberalism in capitalism, Protestantism and individualism.[40] So, in the end, they become not really separate traditions, but liberal subsets. And Smith's emphasis on how issues of race, ethnicity and gender cannot be neatly subsumed into the Tocquevillian/Hartzian thesis is well taken. For much of American history many groups have been "shut out" of participation in the Lockean liberal game, but the members of these various groups still were exposed to American culture and were, therefore, "latent liberals," waiting for the opportunity to participate. Indeed, in recent decades, the liberal arena has widened to accommodate, more and more and to an increasing extent, those that were denied access. The formerly excluded then tend to engage in liberal conduct. Nonetheless, Smith is right in emphasizing how "ascriptive traditions" have always existed alongside Lockean liberalism in America. But they should be comprehended more as examples of waning communitarian capital, fading gradually, like family and church, before the unremitting expansion of the liberal Self.

In the end, other approaches all become finally ancillary to Hartz's liberal thesis. Roelofs' and Hofstadter's cooptation of Calvin, for example, neatly blends him into the liberal matrix, while Abbot's biblical tradition, proposed as a counter-tradition to liberalism, is best understood, instead, as the religious off-shoot of the core American individualist idea.

IV

Locke and Hobbes, then, inevitably predominate in America and, as individualism expands, Lockean government flirts with Hobbesian solutions while society comes to resemble, more and more, the war of all against all. But, governmentally, Hobbes must always work within Lockean constitutional parameters whereas he is not so bound societally. Lockean self-restraint works on the governmental level but not necessarily in society. Locke, though, wanted both government *and* one's neighbors restrained, relying on a combination of constitutional limits, political power and assumed societal control. But as societal control over the Self fades, extant constitutional limits guard against the acquisition and centralization of enough political power to counterbalance the loss of self-restraint. Locke's original balance is hence in jeopardy as government becomes more and more unable to protect us against our neighbors, while at the same time threatening potentially everyone's basic protection against overweening, intrusive governmental power.

The key would appear to be a revitalization of societally instructed self-restraint, but the problem here is that accomplishing such a goal involves essentially putting the genie back into the bottle. Self-restraint works on the basis of the idea that a certain course of action is ruled off-limits by a conscience informed by sets of rules that are unconsciously or unquestioningly accepted. Once one acquires the habit of doing as one wishes and it is realized that the sun, moon and stars do not fall on one's head, at least not immediately, when one does so, then the imposed taboo is shaken, if not altogether shattered. In biblical language, once you realize you can sin and get away with it, the fear of the unknown consequence has been shelved. This would then lead to a further, perhaps constant, pushing against more and more layers of limits. It is indeed difficult to return to self-restraint when the idea of self-expansion has become the only real value left —

and one that has become habitually experienced while continually, of course, bemoaned by a residual Protestant conscience. It is almost as if the *lack* of self-restraint has become the new, real societal value, reinforced always by a brazenly acquisitive capitalist culture and its principal agent of socialization, the media. Family, church, school and neighborhood, in this context, have little chance to impose countervailing communitarian values. Other becomes more and more reified and the cultivation of empathy dissipates.

Thus, the Hobbesian description of conflictual human behavior portrayed in *Leviathan* has come to be more and more realized in America. Hobbes's comprehension of the condition of man, unflinchingly grasped at the start of the liberal tradition, seems to be more appropriate than ever. In this regard, the four American writers discussed in this text all intuitively foresaw this development, however inchoately. They could see where our Hobbesian-Lockean roots were directing us and, in effect, in their work, they anticipate our problem of excessive individualism today, even though three of them wrote in the 19th century and one of them in the beginning decades of the 20th. The clarity and complexity of their cultural analysis, expressed in their insightful works, are the subjects of the next four chapters.

Notes

1. Louis Hartz, *The Liberal Tradition in America* (New York: Harcourt, Brace and World, 1955), 6.
2. See, for example, H Mark Roelofs, *The Poverty of American Politics* (Philadelphia: Temple University Press, 1992); Donald J. Devine, *The Political Culture of the United States* (Boston: Little, Brown, 1972); Daniel J. Boorstein, *The Genius of American Politics* (Chicago: University of Chicago Press, 1953); Alexis de Tocqueville, *Democracy in America* ed. J.P. Meyer (New York: Harper and Row, 1969); Gunnar Myrdal, *An American Dilemma* (New York: Harper and Row, 1944); William T. Bluhm, *Theories of the Political System*, 3rd ed. (Englewood Cliffs, N.J.: Prentice-Hall, 1978), 317-324; Richard Hofstadter, *The American Political Tradition* (New York: Random House, 1948); John Patrick Diggins, *The Lost Soul of American Politics: Virtue, Self-Interest and the Foundations of Liberalism* (Chicago: University of Chicago, 1984); Joshua Foa Dienstag, "Serving God and Mammon: The Lockean Sympathy in Early American Thought," *American Political Science Review* 90, no. 3 (September, 1996): 497-511; Robert N. Bellah et al., *Habits of the Heart* (New York: Harper and Row, 1985); Christopher Lasch, *The Culture of Narcissism* (New York: Norton, 1979); Philip Slater, *The Pursuit of Loneliness* (Boston: Beacon, 1970); Mason Drukman, *Community and Purpose in America* (New York: McGraw-Hill, 1971); Herbert McClosky and John Zaller, *The American Ethos* (Cambridge, Mass.: Harvard University Press, 1984); Samuel Huntington, *American Politics: The Promise of Disharmony* (Cambridge, Mass.: Harvard University Press, 1981); and Garry Wills, *Nixon Agonistes: The Crisis of the Self-Made Man* (New York: New American Library, 1969).
3. John Locke, *Second Treatise on Government* (New York: Liberal Arts Press, 1952).
4. David M. Potter, *People of Plenty: Economic Abundance and the American Character* (Chicago: University of Chicago Press, 1954).
5. See C.B. Macpherson, *The Political Theory of Possessive Individualism* (Oxford: Oxford University Press, 1962); Frank Coleman, "The Hobbesian Basis of American Constitutionalism," *Polity* 7, no. 1 (Fall, 1974): 57-89; and Leo Strauss, *Natural Right and History* (Chicago: University of Chicago Press, 1953).
6. Thomas Hobbes, *Leviathan*, ed. Michael Oakshott (New York: Collier, 1962), 103.
7. Ibid., 100.
8. Genesis 16.12.
9. In making this argument, David Easton echoes Hobbes.
10. Hobbes, *Leviathan*, 98.

11. Ibid., 99.
12. Ibid.
13. Ibid., 100.
14. ibid., 131.
15. Ibid., 103.
16. Ibid., 123.
17. Ibid., 103.
18. This is, of course, one of Locke's principal arguments.
19. On this matter, both Strauss and Macpherson agree.
20. William Shakespeare, *King Lear*, act 3, scene 4.
21. Hofstadter, *The American Political Tradition*, 3.
22. Ibid., 16.
23. Robert D. Putnam, "Bowling Alone: America's Declining Social Capital," *Journal of Democracy* 6, no. 1 (January, 1995):65-78.
24. See Richard M. Huber, *The American Idea of Success* (New York: McGraw-Hill, 1971).
25. Alexis de Tocqueville, *Democracy in America*, ed. Richard D. Heffner (New York: Mentor, 1956), 229.
26. Ibid., 193.
27. Ibid., 194.
28. Roelofs, *The Poverty of American Politics*, 24.
29. Ibid., 40. As Hofstadter writes, the Founders established a system "based upon the philosophy of Hobbes and the religion of Calvin," assuming that "the natural state of mankind is a state of war, and that the carnal mind is at enmity with God." *The American Political Tradition*, 3.
30. Daniel Bell has pointed out this collision between capitalism and the self-restrain of Protestant morality. See the *Cultural Contradictions of Capitalism* (New York: Basic Books, 1976).
31. Roelofs, *The Poverty of American Politics*, 42.
32. See George Thayer, *The Farther Shores of Politics* (New York: Simon and Shuster, 1968).
33. See Amitai Etzioni, "A Moderate Communitarian Proposal," *Political Theory* 24, no. 2 (May, 1996): 155-171; and *Community and Morality* (New York: Basic Books, 1997).
34. Will Kymlicka, *Liberalism, Community and Culture* (Oxford: Clarendon Press, 1989), 10.
35. For two classic communitarian studies see Michael Sandel, *Liberalism and the Limits of Justice* (New York: Cambridge University Press, 1982); and Alasdair MacIntyre, *After Virtue* (Notre Dame, Ind.: University of Notre Dame Press, 1981).
36. By the term "expanded Hartzian thesis" I am referring to Hartz, Roelofs and Coleman.
37. See, e.g. the civic republican argument of J.G.A. Pocock, *The Machiavellian Moment* (Princeton, N.J.: Princeton University Press, 1975); and Garry Will's thesis that the Founders were strongly influenced

by Scottish philosophy in *Inventing America* (Garden City, N.Y.: Doubleday, 1978).
38. See Philip Abbott, *Political Thought in America* (Itasca, Illinois: F.E. Peacock, 1991); and Rogers M. Smith, "Beyond Tocqueville, Myrdal and Hartz: The Multiple Traditions in America," *American Political Science Review* 87, no.3 (September, 1993):549-566.
39. Diggins clearly makes this case in *The Lost Soul of American Politics*.
40. Abbott, *Political Thought in America*, 2.

Chapter 3
ಏಾಡ
The Scarlet Letter

I

The Scarlet Letter is a powerful tale of the complexities and dynamics of American individualism and is "now fully accepted as Hawthorne's masterpiece."[1] It is a story of three main characters, each of which is locked, virtually from first to last, in a unique separate world. In the course of the novel, motivated by the intense connective emotion of love or hate, one or the other tries to pierce the discrete world of another self, but ultimately to no avail. At the end, each is alone, dying apart in her/his own world — even Dimmesdale, who allows himself only minimal final comfort in the arms of Hester. Hester's, Dimmesdale's and Chillingworth's positive and negative efforts to transcend their separation only bring about destruction in the end, although Hester's and Dimmesdale's isolation is relieved by some few moments of physical and emotional intimacy.

The three characters are really walled into autonomous worlds, cut off from each other both physically and psychologically. The number of revealed meetings between Hester and Dimmesdale are few and far between and all the characters' perceptions of each other's wants and needs are almost always divergent and conflictual.

Nonetheless, they persist in their efforts to transcend their egoistic aloneness. The novel is really about these efforts and their inevitable failure. The ultimate lesson of this novel, then, written in the mid-19th century with its setting in 17th century Boston, is that Americans have always been about the same project. We have always been unable to transcend our walled egos — and so we collide. Hawthorne and Melville had the greatest of these collisions, the Civil War, forced immediately on their attention, but the Civil War is just the most bloody and egregious of these confrontations. Misunderstandings, conflict, isolation and yearning are at the heart of the American, Hobbesian-Lockean experience and have always been so.

In *The Scarlet Letter*, in this brief but powerful and poignant tale, Hawthorne concisely addresses these values that underlie American sociopolitical experience. He also suggests how to transcend them through a form of tragic acceptance and reconciliation.

II

Recognized as one of the greatest novels in American literature, *The Scarlet Letter* has been critiqued and debated from multiple perspectives. In an early review, in 1851, Arthur Cleveland Coxe wrote that "*The Scarlet Letter* has already done not a little to degrade our literature and to encourage social licentiousness."[2] He referred to the novel as a "misstep" by Hawthorne and hoped that Hawthorne's future career would redeem him from his mistakes. What bothered Coxe was the author's lack of a straightforward moral condemnation of Hester and Dimmesdale. In general, however, the novel was well received and regarded as a masterful piece of writing, albeit it was often perceived as an extremely gloomy work.[3] It was Herman Melville though, who immediately realized what Hawthorne was really doing and praised him for the profundity of the novel, writing in Hawthorne's defense that his friend "is immeasurably deeper than the plummet of the mere critic."[4] Melville added that it was "that blackness in Hawthorne . . . that so fixes and fascinates me."[5] And well it would, for the same capacity for "blackness," for comprehending the dark side of the American character, was, of course, highly developed in Melville also.[6] This was the basis of their literary and personal friendship. Hawthorne even worried if he had gone too far, if he had been so unremitting in his dark and complex probing of the American soul that the novel would fail to win at least a measure of popularity. He was proven wrong in this concern, although Melville *would* fail to find a mass audience with the perhaps even more profound and "black" *Moby-Dick.*

Critical appreciation of the problem that lies at the heart of the American culture has never. of course, been a mass activity. Many literary analysts, however, have always known what *The Scarlet Letter* is really all about. In 1904, in the aptly titled essay, "The Solitude of Nathaniel Hawthorne," Paul Elmer More wrote that Hawthorne's voice is

> an intensification of the solitude that invests the modern world, and by right found its deepest expression in the New England heart. Not with impunity had the human race for ages dwelt on the eternal welfare of the soul; for from such meditation the sense of personal importance had become exacerbated to an extraordinary degree. What could result from such teaching as that of Jonathan Edwards but an extravagant sense of individual existence, as if the moral governance of the world revolved about the action of each mortal soul?[7]

More goes on to say that Western individualism had been pursued for centuries in the context of Christianity and that transcendentalism was really a 19th century version of the Christian idea. But, in Hawthorne's time, these consoling metaphysical supports for individualism began to pale and fade[8] and this resulted necessarily in

> a feeling of anguish and bereavement more tragic than any previous moral stage through which the world had passed. The loneliness of the individual, which had been vaguely felt and lamented by poets and philosophers of the past, took on a poignancy altogether unexpected. It needed but an artist with the vision of Hawthorne to represent this feeling as the one tragic calamity of moral life, as the great primeval curse of sin. What lay dormant in the teaching of Christianity became the universal protest of the human heart.[9]

So, for More, Hawthorne's greatness is entwined with his being present at the creation, so to speak. He realized that Hawthorne's sensitive genius was attuned to the beginning of the decoupling of American individualism from the assuaging balm of Christianity. The self was more alone than ever now, and Hawthorne was intuitively aware of this. Hawthorne could see where American culture was going, although he almost assuredly could not have fully imagined the extent to which individualism has intensified today. He knew, though, that transcendentalism was shallow[10] and that it was probably the last best gasp of traditional religious affirmation for his time.[11]

The Scarlet Letter is so powerful, then, and critical for this study, because Hawthorne invented it at the moment when he intuitively realized that individualism in America was clearly emerging as if from *bas-relief*, when it was being compelled to stand stark and alone, without any ultimate soothing support. Hawthorne knew individualism was here and here to stay. We had created it in the West and it was now all we really had in America in terms of a cultural anchor. In the end, his awareness of this jarring reality would lead him to fall back upon that which has always been the final recourse for Western alienation — the tragic perspective.

More continues in his essay and adds that we may "count it among the honours" of our American literature" that it was left for a denizen of this far Western land, living in the midst of a later born and confused civilization," to give us "the most perfect utterance of a feeling that must seem to us now as old and as deep as life itself."[12] And, indeed, that to which More refers, the tragic impulse, does go back to our beginnings, to Job and Oedipus. Hawthorne's brilliance lies in seeing how the self will be more alone now than ever in modernity and in immediately linking the stranded self with the tragic tradition of Western literature.

It is this tragic interpretation of *The Scarlet Letter* that I would further develop here. Hawthorne derives the isolation of the characters from, of course; their American situation which tends to exacerbate the individualistic aspect of human nature. The implication is that full awareness of the necessity and inevitability of this individuation leads, in its highest form, to the vision of tragedy.[13]

Certainly, the tragic dimension of *The Scarlet Letter* has been argued extensively before.[14] Seymour Gross has stated that "What is significant in *The Scarlet Letter* is not that Hester is right or wrong in an absolute sense, but rather that she has integrity in her own terms, that she has fallen in love with a minister who has integrity in different terms, and that therefore their love is condemned to be mangled in the clash of their ultimately irreconcilable moralities."[15] Their isolation from each other, fostered by the starkly individualistic sociopolitical philosophy of their culture, results in their being immersed in "the permanence and mystery of human suffering," an experience "basic to the tragic sense of life."[16] Through suffering, Hester, at least, comes to be at peace, accepting the incompleteness that lies at the heart of human life. She is thrown back upon herself, into a condition essential to the nature of being human. In the end, she has no "isms" or "ologies" to protect or comfort her or to give purpose and order to her life. She is profoundly alone. The human desire for fulfillment, for transcendence, has not been satisfied. For her, there is only acceptance and resignation.

Other Western cultures have tapped into this sensibility from different avenues. For Job and Oedipus and Lear, it is the collapse of the organizing principles of their civilizations that compels them to face the primal terror. For Americans, though, it is the awareness of the ultimate failure of egoistic individualism to satisfy our deepest needs, to allow us to bridge the gap between Self and Other, that leads to tragic knowledge. Hawthorne understood this and he made *The Scarlet Letter* his finest and most profound example of the limits of improper self-involvement.

Of course, such a reading of *The Scarlet Letter* is only one of many possible ways to understand the novel. There have been many stages and trends in Hawthorne criticism. Hawthorne was critiqued for being too personally isolated,[17] which resulted in his excessive gloominess,[18] for being immoral, and for provincialism.[19] His writings have also been subject to the realist-idealist debate[20] and a number of works have focused on his use of symbolism in the nineteenth century.[21] In recent years, important work on *The Scarlet Letter* has been done utilizing such perspectives as formalism or the "new criticism,"[22] psychoanalytic criticism,[23] reader-response criticism,[24] feminist criticism,[25] deconstruction,[26] the new historicism,[27] and phenomenological criticism.[28] There seems to be no end as to what can be said about his novels and stories.

But, again, in terms of the above, the preferred approach here is to root Hawthorne in his awareness of the nature of excessive individualism, connecting him thereby with the longstanding tragic view of *The Scarlet Letter* and the post formalist emphasis on fundamental themes in great literature.[29] As a result, we can derive from *The Scarlet Letter* that the implications for politics of intensive Hobbesian-Lockean individualism lie in the responsibilities and consolations of the tragic perspective.

III

It is not surprising that Hawthorne should lace the themes of individualist isolation and tragedy throughout *The Scarlet Letter* since he had personal experience of an America peopled by starkly individualistic egos. He knew too that he was very much one of them. As he looked at himself and his immediate family, human isolation appeared at every hand. In an autobiographical note dating from 1853 he remarked that "I had always a natural tendency . . . toward seclusion . . . and this I now indulged to the utmost."[30] Always, "isolation is one of his major themes."[31] He resolutely held "his (own) individuality inviolate,"[32] although he was by no means a recluse. Actually, "Though isolation was not *in literal fact* of great moment in Hawthorne's life, he gave it great importance in speaking about himself. . . . In keeping with his habit of seeing mankind represented in himself, he exaggerated the depth of his isolation as a sort of metaphorical statement of his views on man in relation to his fellow men."[33] (Italics mine)

This concept of the isolated self is found throughout Hawthorne's work "from the first to the last,"[34] not just in *The Scarlet Letter*. His short stories often "picture a character alone or at the edge of a crowd."[35] His story "Wakefield, " for example, written in 1835, is about a married man who left home as usual one day and did not return for twenty years, all the while living in disguise on the street next to his own house. When he returned, he "entered the door one evening, quietly, as from a day's absence and became a loving spouse till death."[36] Hawthorne makes clear that Wakefield never had a "shadow of a reason for such self-banishment."[37] Then why did he do it? Hawthorne does not provide a definitive explanation, but it is inferred that either through whim or fate or perversity, Wakefield flirted with the ever-present human tendency to immerse in complete egocentricity and then became a victim of his own devolved creation. "A morbid vanity . . . (lay) at the bottom of the affair,"[38] Hawthorne wrote. Clearly, too, he disapproves of Wakefield's behavior. Wakefield is referred to as a "nincompoop"[39] and a "fool."[40] In Hawthorne's words, Wakefield had failed to appreciate that "It is perilous to make a chasm in human affections."[41]

Wakefield had indulged in the American disease, in excessive, egocentric individualism, which not only brought grief and suffering to family and friends, but, in turning him in upon himself, cut him off from transcendent opportunity. To be so alone cannot bring happiness and, indeed, Wakefield, during those twenty years of isolation, gives no evidence of being a happy man.[42]

But the strangeness of the tale reveals much about Hawthorne and his attitude towards the alienated self. In the story, as "in the later stories and the four novels . . . isolation appears again and again as either cause or effect of guilt."[43] Pride or self-indulgence or the failure to perform some commonly accepted human obligation or the violation of another's privacy all bring nothing but pain and misery on the perpetrator.

So we are all alone, but we must not accept this as final, Hawthorne suggests. We must reach out to others and be ever so careful not to damage the fragile bonds of affection that connect us to others. We should be grateful for whatever connective we have established and be sensitive not to damage it, for we are always so perilously close to tumbling back down into isolated self-consciousness. Perhaps it is only an illusory bond that ever connects us to others, but it is critically valuable nonetheless. Our happiness, our sanity and, by implication, the survival of our society, depend on these tenuous connective cords.

At one point, in his solitude, Wakefield "cries out, passionately, 'Wakefield! Wakefield! You are mad!'"[44] And surely we would be mad to jeopardize our only chance to reach beyond the prison boundaries of the self. After all, "Amid the seeming confusion of our mysterious world, individuals are so nicely adjusted to a system, and systems to one another and to a whole that, by stepping aside for a moment, a man exposes himself to a fearful risk of losing his place forever. Like Wakefield, he may become, as it were, the Outcast of the Universe."[45] The inevitable atomized self in American society is always in danger of slipping into a solipsistic egotism that does damage to others because it fails to see others as autonomous entities also. It fails to seriously try to transcend itself. Ultimately, a real attempt at transcendence means that one accepts the perpetual apartness of others as a given and then tries to connect in spite of the inevitability of failure. Such an approach would result in the least social damage, the least collision with others. This interpersonal strategy, however, is expressly what the main characters in *The Scarlet Letter* fail to do and thus hangs Hawthorne's cautionary tale.

IV

Hester is clearly the central character in Hawthorne's great novel, a position well supported by contemporary feminist criticism.[46] And the author makes it very clear from the start that he wants Hester to be considered in relation to the thought and activities of Anne Hutchinson. At the beginning of the novel, for example, Hester is confined to the same prison in which the "sainted Anne Hutchinson"[47] had earlier been detained. In a later chapter Hester is explicitly linked with the Puritan dissident. Hawthorne writes that, if not for Pearl, and Hester's sense of responsibility towards her, "She might have come down to us in history, hand in hand with Anne Hutchinson, as the foundress of a religious sect. She might, in one of her phases, have been a prophetess. She might, and not improbably would, have suffered death from stern tribunals of the period for attempting to undermine the foundations of the Puritan establishment."[48] So Hester has much in common with her predecessor.

Clearly, Hester and Hutchinson are threats to Puritan order because both are representative of the idea of fully autonomous individualism. The Puritans, as critics of the Anglican tradition, which they thought to be too similar to Catholicism and too repressive of the individual conscience, were also ostensibly individualists, but they had come to believe, in the New World, that they had found the ideal balance between the individual and the community. When Hutchinson, in her antinomian position, argued for "only a purer form of Calvinism," for a "totally self-sufficient private illumination,"[49] however, the Puritan elite believed she went too far and moved against her. In fact, however, she was only correcting the tendency of an emerging Protestant orthodoxy "to conflate the visible with the invisible church" and to institutionalize its authority.[50] She was really bringing Puritanism back to its original principles. But, in so doing, she jeopardized the imposed status quo. By acting the way it did, though, in a culture even nominally individualist, the Puritan establishment really was asking for trouble, since, in a liberal society, if "the community overextends and mystifies its authority, the individual will trust the deepest passional self to nullify it all."[51] The Quakers had made the same essential argument in a more sectarian form.

For Hawthorne, both Hutchinson and Hester are representative of spiritual freedom. He knew that, in America, we are *all* really antinomians. Just as Hutchinson did not believe that the truly saved should be subject to any man-made law but should, instead, rely on their own inner vision of truth, so Hester, in the end, becomes a law unto herself. Excluded from society, she turns further in upon herself. Always strong-willed and independent, she becomes even more autonomous because of her enforced seclusion. Yet, she does try to accommodate herself to the strictures and rules of the community. She accepts that she had sinned but, equally, she is "unable to transcend her heartfelt conviction that she (had) not sinned."[52] Relying inevitably on her own inner compass, she knows she loves Dimmesdale and she knows she loves Pearl, the product of the act of transgression. With her heart as moral guide, she can still convince herself, though, that the community is at least partially right. By wearing the scarlet letter and remaining in Boston, she indicates that she accepts responsibility for what she has done, but when she tries convincingly to inculcate the group's judgment, to adopt it fully as her own, she finds she can not do it. It does not, in the end, wholly ring true to her. And, since, as a good Protestant, she has to depend, finally, on her own conscience, she has no other recourse but to trust her own resolve and not the presumed wisdom of the Boston community.

> Isolation had been the key for Hester. It had intensified her individualism. Standing alone in the world, — alone, as to any dependence on society, and with little Pearl to be guided and protected, — alone, and hopeless of retrieving her position, even had she not scorned to consider it desirable, — she cast away the fragments of a broken chain. The world's law was no law for her mind. It was an age in which the human intellect, newly emancipated, had taken a more active and wider range than for many centuries before. Men of the sword had overthrown nobles and kings. Men bolder than these had overthrown and rearranged — not actually, but within the sphere of theory, which was their most real abode — the whole system of ancient prejudice, wherewith was linked much ancient principle. Hester Prynne imbibed this spirit. She assumed a freedom of speculation, then common enough on the other side of the Atlantic, but which our forefathers, had they known of it, would have held to be a deadlier crime than that stigmatized by the scarlet letter. In her lonesome cottage, by the seashore, thoughts visited her, such as dared to enter no other dwelling in New England.[53]

Her apparent acceptance of her punishment and her accommodating deportment disguise her inner turbulence. As Hawthorne writes,

"It is remarkable," after all, "that persons who speculate the most boldly often conform with the most perfect quietude to the external regulations of society. The thought suffices them, without investing itself in the flesh and blood of action."[54]

True to her own personalist affirmation, Hester does not act, in the end, to bring about general reform as did Ann Hutchinson, but, instead, she acts to attempt to resolve her complex personal relationship with both Dimmesdale and the Boston community. This is why she considered fleeing with Dimmesdale and Pearl to Europe. She believes that, by doing do, she can bring peace, happiness and resolution to her own life as well as live freely with those she loves.

In this sense, Hester is even more of an individualist than Hutchinson, for Hester feels "particular obligations to human beings far more than she feels general social responsibilities." This is "appropriate to her role as representative of individual and personal, rather than social, power. A reformer is dedicated to social power and has abandoned an individual center. No doubt this makes the whole issue of social reform on behalf of individualism highly problematic; so far as Hester is concerned — and this is our concern at present — the very consistency of her individualism keeps her within the sphere of the personal."[55]

She does not start a new religion — or try to. She believes she has a private problem and she wants a private solution. At the end of the story, she is prepared to let Heaven, in its own time, reveal "a new truth . . . in order to establish the whole relation between man and woman on a surer ground of mutual happiness,"[56] if such a foundation exists. She has tried to find this answer in her own life but she is resigned to her loss, she is not despondent. Without hope of happiness, she continues to reach to and comfort others and to believe wanly in the possibilities of mankind's future. At the conclusion, having "no selfish ends"[57] and yet more self-contained than ever, she is aware of the tragic, unbridgeable space between herself and all else. She achieves a dark wisdom that allows her to appreciate human frailty and fallibility and the sad ironies and ambiguities of men's and women's goals and desires. She has attained a degree of detachment. Thus, in becoming a more profoundly autonomous self, Hester touches the depths of the tragic tradition. Tragic acceptance is her final consolation, achieved, classically, through great personal suffering.

V

And there is much suffering to go around. Hester is not the only one ensconced in individualist confinement. Dimmesdale and Chillingworth are equally unable to transcend their aloneness. The main difference between her and them, however, is that they are destroyed by their isolation, and by their failed attempts to deal with it, without experiencing any comprehension of their real situation, without realizing a more profound dimension to their atomism. Because of the passage of time and also, principally, because of her own deep and complex nature, she comes to have an understanding of life that the two men never grasp.

Hester's struggle is to reconcile her inner and outer selves and, while the tale "clearly embodies the authorial realization that inner and outer can never be completely congruent,"[58] she does, in the end, achieve an essential tragic acceptance of the space between public and private.

Dimmesdale, however, is literally destroyed by his inability to bring his inner self into line with Puritan ideology. For him, assertions of individuality, of autonomous will, can only be negative. In his mind, without the constraint of the community's ideology, we devolve into vicious selfishness — and to fail once, to open the door a crack, is to risk letting all of human evil rush out. When he accepts Hester's entreaty in the forest and plans to escape with her, he comes to believe that this would be the end of all restraint. On the walk back from the forest, he frightens himself with his negative individuality. "At every step he was incited to do some strange, wild, wicked thing or other, with a sense that it would be at once involuntary and intentional, — in spite of himself, yet growing out of a profounder self than that which opposed the impulse."[59] He thinks to himself that he is now "given over utterly to the fiend" who suggests "the performance of every wickedness which the most foul imagination can conceive."[60] By the time he returns to his dwelling he realizes that his former self was gone, that "another man had returned out of the forest, a wiser one, with a knowledge of hidden mysteries which the simplicity of the former never could have reached." He has achieved "a bitter kind of knowledge."[61]

But he has not really broadened his understanding of himself or attained real insight into the human condition in general. He has just confirmed his original ideological presupposition that the self, without rigid repression and self-restraint, would devolve into pure evil. So he has a simple answer to the Self-Other problem, viz. abnegate the self. This comes to him as a revelation, as wisdom, and so he feels his course is clear. He will reject escape with Hester and confess his sin to all. He couldn't do it earlier because his sense of himself was completely wrapped up with his perfectionist ideology and his advocacy of it. If he confessed his personal failure, his self, he believed, would have been lost, so he had tried to punish himself privately, slowly destroying himself physically. For years, this was all he felt he could do. In effect, "The only truth that continued to give Mr. Dimmesdale a real existence on this earth was the anguish in his inmost soul, and the undissembled expression of it in his aspect."[62] But, in the end, confession and death become the only route to finally preserving his integrity. To escape with Hester, or to confess and try to carry on, will equally destroy him in his conception of himself as an individual. His believes sincerely that the self, without the most massive acceptance of societal restraint, is satanic and will destroy civility, society, and civilization. By confessing and dying on the scaffold, he, in effect, gives his greatest sermon of all and dies at peace, at one with his own view of himself.

Dimmesdale, thus, self-destructs, when he could have escaped with Hester sooner or later. But if he is defeated by excessive self-restraint, then Chillingworth is finally destroyed by a complete lack of any real restraint. His problem, directly diametric to Dimmesdale's, is excessive selfishness. He wants revenge, plain and simple. He had been wronged and he wants his pound of flesh. He is an intelligent and learned man, which makes his evil all the worse, for he uses his talents for the most devious purposes. In his desire to destroy the minister, he is unlimited by any mercy or self-doubt. As a man of reason and science, he is not restrained by Puritan religion. He is a loner and concerned only about himself. Even though he knows that he probably started the whole train of events by wanting Hester to marry him in the first place, even though he knows it was not an appropriate marriage since Hester never loved him, he does not restrain his selfish intentions.

Not so ironically, it is his very aloneness that accounts for his egocentric, sadistic behavior. He wants to stay in Boston and pursue his evil intent because he is not happy in his alienation. He finds himself compelled to relate, to connect with others, and if he can not do so in a positive way, then he is determined to do so negatively. As he says, "Here, on this wild outskirt of earth, I shall pitch my tent, for, elsewhere a wanderer, and isolated from human interests, I find here a woman, a man, a child, amongst whom and myself there exist the closest ligaments. No matter whether of love or hate; no matter whether of right or wrong! Thou and thine, Hester Prynne, belong to me. My home is where thou art, and where he is."[63]

A sad sort of community this, but it is all Chillingworth believes he has. And the more he is concerned only about his own self, the darker and more intense his negative community becomes. He actually makes plans to go with Hester and Dimmesdale if they flee and, later, in the end, when this fails to come to pass and the minister dies, thereby rending asunder Chillingworth's negative community, the physician "withered up, shriveled away, and almost vanished form mortal sight,"[64] eventually dying within the year.

Neither man, then, grows in wisdom; neither comes, in his personal life or in his relation to Other, to achieve any realistic balance between self and community. Chillingworth's great sin has been to dig "into the poor clergyman's heart like a miner digging for gold," to violate the autonomy of another for the purpose of self-aggrandizement and enjoyment. "Alas for his own soul," [65] Hawthorne writes, for, in the end, we cannot play zero-sum games with others without ultimately destroying ourselves. Chillingworth, in his excessive egoistic conduct, is "striking evidence of man's faculty of transforming himself into a devil, if he will only, for a reasonable space of time, undertake a devil's office."[66] To be really evil, then, to be really satanic, in Hawthorne's mind, is to relate to others without any self-restraining capacity, any concern for that desirable balance between Self and Other.

Neither Dimmesdale nor Chillingworth, really, has any sense of this balance. Both Dimmesdale's self-abnegation and Chillingworth's excessive concern with self has resulted in their self-destruction. Neither has managed to evolve any appropriate societal Self-Other equipoise. In tilting too far to one side or the other of the equation, they conjointly fail to properly address the needs of individual or community. Too much self is not the answer, suggests Hawthorne, but neither is too little.

VI

It is Hester, then, who incorporates Hawthorne's conception of a Self-Other balance by embracing the lessons of tragedy — and this is done only through experience, disillusionment and suffering. Chillingworth and Dimmesdale have been guilty of sin, and so has Hester, but Hester's sin is different. Hers is a mistake rooted in an initial misperception of the human condition.

Hawthorne interprets sin as "simply the desire to be independent of others and of the world, expressed in demands which are only the insistence that others submit to the will and desire of the self."[67] However, Hester's mistake, rooted in her need to transcend the self in love for another, is to fail to appreciate the difference between the minister and herself. They are really in different worlds. Whereas Hester puts her faith in the individual's capacity to expand, develop and love, Dimmesdale, with much less imagination, roots himself in stock Puritan ideology. Hester assumes that what is good for her is good for him also, but, in fact, by causing him to doubt the ground of his being, she destroys him. The escape plan, hatched in the forest, ("A Flood of Sunshine"), could never have worked. Dimmesdale could never have been happy outside of Massachusetts — and he could no longer be happy in the Boston colony because he had violated his moral code with Hester. It is only at the end, after Dimmesdale's death, that Hester intuitively realizes how really alone she has always been. Even though isolated and shunned in the village, she has always cherished her special, unspoken connection with the minister. Now she knows she has completely misunderstood both him and their relationship. They can never be together — not even in death.

Her love, then, is really an unconscious attempt to selfishly impose her *weltanschauung* on Dimmesdale. She is an extraordinary person, highly self-reliant and far ahead of her time, as was Ann Hutchinson, but Dimmesdale is far less creative, adaptable and self-confident. In effect, and, of course, without so intending, she has really overwhelmed and destroyed him.

Finally, after all the suffering, in the depth of her sadness and defeat, she is able to appreciate the inevitable distance that had always existed between herself and Dimmesdale as being emblematic of all human relations. She implicitly comes to realize that we are not happy alone and we can never be fully together with Other. Dimmesdale's ideological answer to alienation and Chillingworth's crude selfishness got them nowhere, but Hester's belief in her love and in her own creative independence proved to be a failure also. The wisdom of tragic experience, then, is that there are no easy routes to follow, no clear answers to the Self-Other problem.

So, to a close and scrupulous observer like Hawthorne, it must ever be. The pathway is beset with pitfalls and dubious choices. The shrewd pick their way warily. The passionate are likely to stumble or go wrong, and 'good intentions' have no bearing on the inevitable penalty, which often far exceeds the crime. This is hard, but, to the heroic in heart, no cause for despair. There is wisdom to be won from the fine hammered steel of woe; a flower to be plucked from the rosebush at the prison door 'to relieve the darkening close of a tale of frailty and sorrow.' To relieve, but not to reverse or redeem.[68]

This level of insight can be interpreted as a form of conservatism, but it really taps a much deeper Western resource. Transcending Hobbesian-Lockean liberalism and whatever would pass for conservatism in America, Hawthorne had spun out the liberal idea to the nth degree, found it wanting and had come to rest with tragedy. The Self-Other problem, he had intuitively concluded, could not be resolved in the American context, if at all, either by repressing the Self (Dimmesdale), by granting it free egotistic assertion (Chillingworth) or by a facile uniting of Self and Other through elementary love and self-development (Hester).

At the end of the day, each still remains alone and we are all left with a counsel of caution. We are left with individualism in the American matrix — and it alone cannot save us. So, to Hawthorne, it appears that the best we can do is "direct our energies to the solution of problems of immediate, pragmatic concern as they arise." What Hawthorne does really offer is "what one may label an anti-ideological ideology."[69] He implies that we must muddle through, if we can, as Hester did, who was made wise and balanced through experience and reflective inner growth, two mature qualities often lacking in an American social context of shallow, rapacious individualism.

Notes

1. B. Bernard Cohen, ed., *The Recognition of Nathaniel Hawthorne: Selected Criticism Since 1828* (Ann Arbor: University of Michigan Press, 1969), xiv.
2. Arthur Cleveland Coxe, "The Writings of Hawthorne," *Church Review* 3 (Jan., 1851) in *Recognition of Nathaniel Hawthorne*, ed. Cohen, 52.
3. Edwin Percy Whipple, "Nathaniel Hawthorne," *Atlantic Monthly* 5 (May, 1860) in *Recognition of Nathaniel Hawthorne*, ed. Cohen, 58-70.
4. Herman Melville, "Hawthorne and His Mosses," *Literary World* 7 (17 and 24 August, 1850) in *Recognition of Nathaniel Hawthorne*, ed. Cohen, 33.
5. Ibid.
6. See Randall Stewart, *Nathaniel Hawthorne: A Biography* (Hamden, Connecticut: Archon, 1948); and Hubert H. Hoeltje, "Hawthorne, Melville and 'Blackness,'" *American Literature* (March, 1965) in *Recognition of Nathaniel Hawthorne*, ed. Cohen, 257-267, for a denial of Hawthorne's "blackness."
7. Paul Elmer More, "The Solitude of Nathaniel Hawthorne," *Shelburne Essays*, First Series (New York, 1904) in *Recognition of Nathaniel Hawthorne*, ed. Cohen, 143.
8. Nietzsche had come to essentially the same conclusion at about the same time in mid-19th century Europe.
9. More, "The Solitude of Nathaniel Hawthorne," 143.
10. Emerson, Thoreau and Whitman were all transcendentalists, but Hawthorne and Melville were highly skeptical of it. See John P. Diggins, *The Lost Soul of American Politics* (Chicago: University of Chicago Press, 1984),192-229.
11. For a critique of Hawthorne's skepticism see Vernon L. Parrington, *The Romantic Revolution in America* (New York: Harcourt Brace, 1927), 434-441.
12. More, "The Solitude of Nathaniel Hawthorne," 144.
13. See Richard B. Sewall, *The Vision of Tragedy* (New Haven: Yale University Press, 1980) for an excellent discussion of the tragic tradition.
14. See Sewall, *The Vision of Tragedy*, 86-91; Seymour Gross, "Solitude, and Love, and Anguish: The Tragic Design of *The Scarlet Letter*," in *The Scarlet Letter: Essays in Criticism and Scholarship,* eds. Seymour Gross et.al. (New York: Norton, 1988); George Bailey Loring, review of *The Scarlet Letter*, by Nathaniel Hawthorne, *Massachusetts Quarterly Review* 3 (September 1850): 484-500; F.O. Matthiessen, "Hawthorne's Psychology: The Acceptance of Good and Evil," in *American Renaissance: Art and Expression in the Age of Emerson and Whitman* (London: Oxford University Press, 1941), 337-351; Roy R. Male, *Hawthorne's Tragic Vision* (Austin: University of Texas Press, 1957);

and Anthony Trollope, "The Genius of Nathaniel Hawthorne," *North American Review* 129 (Sept. 1879): 203-233. For a skeptical critique of Hawthorne's tragic depth see Martin Green, *Re-Appraisals: Some Commonsense Readings in American Literature* (New York: Norton, 1965), 61-85 and Lionel Trilling, "Our Hawthorne," in *Hawthorne Centenary Essays,* ed. Roy Harvey Pearce (Columbus: Ohio State University Press, 1964), 429-458.
15. Gross, "Solitude, and Love, and Anguish," 338.
16. Sewall, *The Vision of Tragedy*, 6.
17. See Newton Arvin, *Hawthorne* (Boston: Little, Brown, 1929).
18. Edwin Percy Whipple, "Nathaniel Hawthorne," *Atlantic Monthly* 5 (May, 1980), 614-622.
19. See George Edward Woodberry, *Nathaniel Hawthorne* (Boston: Houghton Mifflin, 1902); and Henry James, *Hawthorne*, English Men of Letters Series (London: Macmillan, 1879).
20. Henry James, for example, criticized *The Scarlet Letter* for not being realistic enough, although he later modified this position. See Trilling, "Our Hawthorne," for a discussion of James' critique.
21. See Woodberry, *Nathaniel Hawthorne*.
22. See F.O. Matthiessen, *American Renaissance: Art and Expression in the Age of Emerson and Whitman*.
23. Frederick C. Crews, *The Sins of the Fathers: Hawthorne's Psychological Themes* (New York: Oxford University Press, 1966).
24. David Leverenz, "Mrs. Hawthorne's Headache: Reading *The Scarlet Letter,*" in *Nathaniel Hawthorne: The Scarlet Letter: Case Studies in Contemporary Criticism,* ed. Ross C. Murfin (Boston: St. Martin's Press, 1991), 263-274.
25. Nina Baym, "The Significance of Plot in Hawthorne's Romances," in *Ruined Eden of the Present: Hawthorne, Melville and Poe,* eds. G.R. Thompson and Virgil Lokke (West Lafayette, Indiana: Purdue University Press, 1981), 49-70.
26. Michael Ragussis, "Silence, Family Discourse and Fiction in *The Scarlet Letter,*" in *Nathaniel Hawthorne: The Scarlet Letter: Case Studies in Contemporary Criticism,* ed. Ross C. Murfin (Boston: St. Martin's Press, 1991), 316-329.
27. Michael Colacurcio, ed., *New Essays on The Scarlet Letter* (Cambridge: Cambridge University Press, 1985).
28. Hugo McPherson, *Hawthorne as Myth-Maker: A Study in Imagination* (Toronto: University of Toronto Press, 1969).
29. See Crews, *The Sins of the Fathers;* and Harry Levin, *The Power of Blackness* (New York: Knopf, 1958).
30. Arlin Turner, *Nathaniel Hawthorne: An Introduction and Interpretation* (New York: Barnes & Noble, 1961), 35.
31. Ibid.
32. Ibid.

33. Ibid., 37.
34. Ibid., 38.
35. Ibid.
36. Nathaniel Hawthorne, "Wakefield," in *The Celestial Railroad and Other Stories*, ed. R. P. Balckmur (New York: New American Library, 1963), 67.
37. Ibid.
38. Ibid., 70.
39. Ibid., 71.
40. Ibid., 72.
41. Ibid., 70.
42. Turner, *Nathaniel Hawthorne: An Introduction and Interpretation*, 39.
43. Ibid.
44. Hawthorne,"Wakefield," 74.
45. Ibid., 75.
46. See Nina Baym, *The Scarlet Letter: A Reading* (Boston: Twayne, 1986).
47. Nathaniel Hawthorne, *The Scarlet Letter* (New York: Alfred A. Knopf, 1992), 50.
48. Ibid., 171.
49. Michael J. Colacurcio, "Footsteps of Ann Hutchinson: the Context of *The Scarlet Letter*," in *The Scarlet Letter: Essays in Criticism and Scholarship,* eds. Gross et.al., 220.
50. Ibid.
51. Ibid.
52. Baym, *The Scarlet Letter: A Reading*, 64.
53. Hawthorne, *The Scarlet Letter*, 170-171.
54. Ibid., 171.
55. Baym, *The Scarlet Letter: A Reading*, 66.
56. Hawthorne, *The Scarlet Letter*, 272-273.
57. Ibid., 272.
58. Colacurcio, "Footsteps," 229-230.
59. Hawthorne, *The Scarlet Letter*, 225.
60. Ibid., 229.
61. Ibid., 231.
62. Ibid., 151.
63. Ibid., 79.
64. Ibid., 269.
65. Ibid., 133.
66. Ibid., 176.
67. Wilson Carey McWilliams, *The Idea of Fraternity in America* (Berkeley: University of California Press, 1973), 308.
68. Sewall,*The Vision of Tragedy,* 91.
69. Jonathan Mendilow, "Nathaniel Hawthorne and Conservatism's 'Night of Ambiguity,'" *Political Theory* 23, no.1 (February, 1995): 142.

Chapter 4

Moby-Dick

Herman Melville's *Moby-Dick* is one of the great masterworks of Western literature and quite probably the greatest American novel. As a product of Western thought it also speaks generally to the human condition as perceived in the West. As a specifically *American* creation, however, as a reflection of the American *weltanschauung*, it should be of particular value in our understanding of ourselves. *Moby-Dick*, in fact, contains rich insights into the American mind, i.e. the Hobbesian-Lockean liberal mind, and is extremely useful to political theorists. Although Melville was not a philosopher and did not specifically, directly, refer to political philosophy, nonetheless the central theme of *Moby-Dick*, "the theme of the individual and his selfhood,"[1] is directly related to the underlying metaphysical assumptions of American political thought. A comprehension of *Moby-Dick* on its most profound level, then, provides not only a deepening of our understanding of the American liberal mind, but also an approach to the management of the serious metaphysical and political problems implied by the monistic American liberal credo.

I

Having divided the world, for each individual, into two parts, Hobbes and Locke assumed that what was "out there," beyond the Self, was to be used by the Self.[2] This presupposes that one can "know" the non-Self, at least to the degree necessary to employ it. However, such an assumption confuses utility with real knowledge, as Hume would demonstrate. Hobbes and Locke simply underestimated the "unknowableness" of Other. Hume recognized this flaw in the liberal tradition[3] and described, in effect, how really isolated the *ens completum* was. It was then left up to Kant to work out a reconciliation between Self and Other, between Hobbes-Locke and Hume, between what we can know and what we cannot know. Kant tried to bring the Self out of the total isolation in which Hume left it, but his solution is far from satisfactory.[4] We are still left with an "unknowable," a noumenal layer of reality from which the Self is forever alienated.

Hence, having drawn out Hobbes and Locke to their deepest metaphysical implications, Hume and Kant left the Self still divided from Other and, really, more alone than before. But if the Self is not *All*, if, that is, there is manifestly more in the world than the Self, unless one assumes solipsism, which liberalism does not, then Other must be taken into account. And, indeed, it is the very presence of Other, the non-Self, that thwarts the Self in its limitless grandiose ambitions and, in the end, claims the Self in death. Ultimately, the non-Self conquers the Self. One's bones and ashes become the non-Self. Other continues after the Self is gone. For all that man is and becomes, then, for all the Self's wisdom and power, in the end, it amounts to nought. The Self, after a life of inevitable pain and suffering, as well as attainment and insight, does not, cannot, triumph. Other, pressing always at the psychic and epithelial boundaries of the Self, overwhelms and conquers. This is man's great tragedy, felt, potentially, all the more painfully by liberal man, by American man, for whom, ostensibly, autonomy is a palpable given. In the end, said Ishmael, "Perhaps at mid-day, in the fairest weather, with one half-throttled shriek you drop through that transparent air into the summer sea, no more to rise forever."[5] You will be gone and "the shroud of the sea" will have "rolled on as it rolled five thousand years ago."[6]

It is this that is ultimately maddening to the liberal Self, particularly to any Self that does not heed Nietzsche's warning and stares into the abyss for too long. For liberal man, the extinction of the Self is the extinction of that which matters most to him, i.e. self-conscious reality. Reason, wisdom, art, virtue avail one not at all in the face of the brute facticity of the non-Self. Ultimately, Other wins. Ultimately, the Self is finished, the Self is over. But why must this be so, thought Ahab. Why should brute, stupid, insensitive non-Self, the great mass of Other, always win? How can this be moral or just? It is evil. It is wrong. Man, in his ethical awareness, is better than Other. Self, in the greatness of human nature, is superior to dumb non-consciousness. Yet Other will win. Self will die. All that man has developed, all his greatest, most creative attainments, are all reduced to emptiness.

Is it all then meaningless? Is the Self, the isolated liberal Self that is up against Other, of no final, cosmic consequence? How can this be if the Self is all that is of importance in liberal theory? Why must the individual die? Why must he be crushed if he is the center of meaning?

II

To these questions, Melville's Ahab, a man of great depth and intellect, provides the answer of defiance. Ahab's autonomous man will not go quietly. He will strike back. He will rage against Other, against Moby-Dick, and thereby show his dignity, man's dignity. He knows that he is doomed, that we are all doomed, but we can refuse to go quietly and not just assume, not just hope, that there is some good, some overall pantheistic or religious purpose in it all.[7] Ahab knows that there is no benevolence in Other because Other is against the Self, the locus of all meaning and value. All that man can do is assert his Self to the last. What else can man, particularly liberal, American man, do — make money, attain property, acquire power? Ahab rejects all of this.[8] This is all too superficial for him. He cuts right to the essence of the whole liberal tradition, right to its metaphysical root, right to that which informs all the superficies of the liberal gestalt. Get to the heart of what it means to be liberal man, he holds. This quest against Other, against Moby-Dick, lies at the center of the whole Hobbesian-Lockean theoretical enterprise.[9]

Ahab is determined to strike at, to conquer, the Ineffable, the "burden of humanity. He faced the darkness as he saw it," determined to go after "whatever it is in nature that . . . oppresses, bewilders and bears man down."[10] Ahab came to identify with Moby-Dick not only all his bodily woes, but all his intellectual and spiritual aspirations. The white whale swam before him as the monomaniac incarnation of all those malicious agencies which some deep men feel eating in them, till they are left living on with half a heart and half a lung. That intangible malignity which has been from the beginning. . . All that most maddens and torments; all that stirs up the lees of things; all truth with malice in it; all that cracks the sinews and cakes the brain; all the subtle demonisms of life and thought; all evils, to crazy Ahab, were visibly personified, and made practically assailable in Moby-Dick. He piled upon the whale's hump the sum of all the general rage and hate felt by his whole race from Adam down; and then, as if his chest had been a mortar, he burst his hot heart's shell upon it.[11]

Ahab saw Moby-Dick as a window that would give him access to what he perceived as the great malignity, to Other, to that which lies behind all things. "All visible objects," he says, in his great speech,

are but as pasteboard masks. But in each event — in the living act, the undoubted deed — there, some unknown but still reasoning thing puts forth the mouldings of its features from behind the unreasoning mask. If man will strike, strike through the mask! How can the prisoner reach outside except by thrusting through the wall? To me, the white whale is that wall, shoved near to me. Sometimes I think there's nought beyond. But 'tis enough. He tasks me; he heaps me; I see in him outrageous strength, with an inscrutable malice sinewing it. That inscrutable thing is chiefly what I hate; and be the white whale agent, or be the white whale principal, I will wreak that hate upon him.[12]

Then he makes clear that he is equal to the task, that Self can and must defeat Other, or, at least, resist it to the death. "Talk to me not of blasphemy, man," he says. "I'd strike the sun if it insulted me. For could the sun do that, then could I do the other; since there is ever a sort of fair play herein, jealousy presiding over all creations. But not my master, man, is even that fair play. Who's over me? Truth hath no confines."[13] Of course, Ahab is referring here to assumed liberal truth.

Ahab, then, takes autonomous Self, liberal man, to the starkest extreme. He pits Self against all of the non-Self, in its entire noumenal reality, which, in Ahab's mind, must be evil because it is against Self. There can be no balance, no *modus vivendi* between the two, no "fair play," for if Self does not resist, Other will eventually win, will in fact win no matter what man does. The two are, in the liberal paradigm, locked in combat. For this reason, Ahab, becoming a figure of Jobian, Promethean, Lear-like dimensions, quests for and strikes at Other, the "all-destroying but unconquering whale."[14] Fighting to the end, spitting his last breath at the whale, Ahab is destroyed in body but not in spirit. His liberal soul remains intact to the end. He has stood up for all individual men, preserving thereby, he believes, the dignity of the autonomous Self. He is still the great tragic hero, fighting for all self-conscious creation, for mankind.

But he is also crazy. Melville makes it very clear that Ahab is mad, that he is not to be emulated.[15] After all, he has destroyed everything, all that he wanted to defend. In his quest to defeat Other, he has only brought ruin upon the Selves, the "isolatoes" of the *Pequod*. He clearly represents individualism gone amok, Hobbesian-Lockean liberalism at its most arrogant. The destruction that follows is the natural result of having an unnatural relationship with the universe. Through Ahab, Melville makes it apparent that the Self cannot conquer Other physically or know Other intellectually. Self and Other are always to be apart. There can be no single interpretation of Other that will allow us to control it. Ahab's monomania, his single vision, is a distortion of Other brought on by his intense Selfness. He is the consummate "isolato," cut off from others and from his own "humanities," walled in by his apartness.

Clearly, Melville uses Ahab to symbolically depict what can happen if self-reliant individualism, Hobbesian-Lockean man, is taken too seriously — particularly in the United States. *Moby-Dick*, after all, is an obviously American book and Melville is obviously addressing the American mind. The ship is named the *Pequod*, one should recall, after the Pequot Indians, a tribe totally crushed by expansive, rapacious American individualism. The ship also carries a crew of thirty — the number of states in the United States at the time the book was written. And Fedallah's prophecy, that Ahab would die only when he sees a hearse on the ocean made of American-grown wood (the *Pequod*, of course), makes it clear that the ship is to be seen as a representative microcosm of America, as well as of the larger world. Indeed, Melville reaches to the center of the American liberal Self and presents its key, inherent problem as essentially a metaphysical and epistemological one. What *is* the Self's relation to Other and what can one know of Other? These queries lie at the core of the American liberal gestalt while, at the same time, they offer the possibility of redemption if they are answered atypically.

III

It is Ishmael who provides Melville's atypical liberal response to liberalism's metaphysical question. Melville makes clear, however, that Ishmael is as much a liberal, as much an "isolato," as is Ahab. The difference is that Ishmael views his Self as being in a developing, balanced relation to Other, one in which Other has its proper, necessary and proportional place, its purpose and its unknowable identity. The problem, for Ishmael, is not one of conquering and subduing Other, as it is for Ahab, but, instead, one of finding the proper relationship to Other. Ahab's view of the evil white whale, Other, "was Ishmael's only when he was immediately under the magnetic spell of the crazed captain."[16] In the chapter "The Whiteness of the Whale," Ishmael discusses how the "secret of the whale is in his whiteness, his lack of color." He explains white "to be a shifting symbol, used at one time for joy and innocence, as at bridals, and for terror and emptiness, as in lepers or polar wastes. White is many things, never one alone." There is, therefore, no single understanding of its meaning. Whiteness and Moby-Dick are then the same — both incomprehensible. Thus, "Ishmael perceives that the White Whale must be left alone; that illusion alone will sustain life."[17]

Whereas Ahab's "great error . . . is (his) failure to accept human limitations," his failure to realize that there is no final truth, no certitude of Self, that he can't, in effect, conquer Other,[18] Ishmael makes no such mistake. Ishmael, too, as intense Self, is on a plane of equality with Other, but he knows he cannot subdue Other — nor does he really wish to. He consistently sees dualities in things, consistently tries not to distort reality through his own perceptions. He tries to let Other be, to let other beings be.[19] In the chapter, "Cetology," Melville implies, through Ishmael, that if one cannot even know all there is to know about whales, how can one possibly know all there is to know about the nature of the universe? How can one be like Ahab? In "The Mast Head," Ishmael, in the rigging, realizes that only at his own peril does he fail to see the ocean, and, in general, all that is below him, symbolic Other, in its own terms. The ocean really is not, emblematically, "the deep, blue, bottomless soul, pervading mankind and nature,"[20] but is, in fact, just itself, just the ocean, into which the Self will fall to its doom if it gets too transported by dream-making. The ocean is not a symbol imposed by the Self on a part of reality but, simply, Other — and it must be respected in its separate opaque integrity or Self will be destroyed.

In the chapter, "The Gilder," Ishmael, Starbuck and Stubb all view the becalmed ocean and attach different meanings to it, but only Ishmael's view is disturbed by doubt. He asks "Where lies the final harbour, whence we unmoor no more? In what rapt ether sails the world, of which the weariest will never weary?" He continues by saying that "Our souls are like those orphans whose unwedded mothers die in bearing them: the secret of our paternity lies in their grave, and we must there to learn it."[21] Ultimate answers are thus not to be found in this life. Starbuck and Stubb engage in interpretations that they regard as absolute, as complete, but not Ishmael. He comes to see that there are no simple, non-complex interpretations.

Melville makes the same point in the chapter, "The Doubloon." Ahab, Starbuck, Stubb, Flask, Fedallah and Pip all separately look at the doubloon that Ahab has nailed to the mainmast. Each finds a different symbolic meaning in the coin. Each determines, for himself, what the coin represents since each thinks that, as Ishmael states, " some certain significance lurks in all things."[22] Just what that significance finally is, though, remains a mystery, since each simply projects his own thoughts upon it. Pip, actually, comes closest to realizing its inscrutable facticity when he comes upon the situation and proclaims, "I look, you look, he looks, we look, ye look, they look."[23] In other words, we all look separately and we all see something different — but yet the object remains noumenally and uniquely itself.

Again and again Melville makes the same point. In "The Town-Ho's Story," in chapters 55, 56, and 57, when he dwells upon the different artistic descriptions of whales, and in "The Tail," "The Prairie," and "The Nut," Melville shows how there can be no simple, direct understanding of anything — all is complex and ultimately unknowable. In reference to trying to know the whale, Ishmael finally confesses that he can only go "skin deep." As he says, "Dissect him how I may, then . . . I know him not and never will."[24]

Ishmael, hence, differs emphatically from Ahab in this very important sense. Ahab sees things, beings, as an extension of himself, of his desire, of his will, albeit unconsciously. *He* is all. He is, in effect, assuming God-like qualities. He is the Self up against and superior to all else. *His* interpretation of anything is the only possible and correct one. His moments of doubt, "his humanities," are overwhelmed by his will, his monomania. Ishmael, on the other hand, makes no such imposition on the world, although he, too, begins the story alone and apart, an "isolato" as much as Ahab. He is also an outcast, true to his name, "a fugitive from society, a man alienated from the normal life of settled communities. Ishmael has no stake in society: he is penniless and apparently without relatives."[25] He too, then, like Ahab, is an alienated Self. He too is American, liberal man, but, because of his metaphysically open-minded approach to fundamental things, an atypical liberal man — and this will make all the difference.

Ishmael's quintessential apartness is certainly intense. He experiences, at the start of the book, a "damp, drizzly November in his soul"[26] and is thinking about suicide. He finds no contentment in a wolfish, sharkish society, as he would describe it, and thus turns to the sea in order to reestablish his bearings. He is in search of the "ungraspable phantom of life,"[27] seemingly knowing intuitively that he can only address his alienation appropriately by seeking a more proper, fundamental, metaphysical balance between his Self and Other. He seems to know that he is out of kilt at the core, at least partially because, he believes, he has been in society, in American society, for too long. He goes to sea, then, as one searches for meaning — out of metaphysical need.

His liberal kinship with Ahab goes only so far, though, for he brings with him a philosophical attitude fundamentally different from Ahab's. Ahab goes to sea in order to conquer, to vanquish the non-Self, whereas Ishmael goes to learn. Ishmael's attitude is an open one, a generous one. He tries to be tolerant of that which he finds different or even dismaying. "I am quick to perceive a horror," he says, "and could still be social with it — would they let me — since it is but well to be on friendly terms with all the inmates of the place one lodges in."[28] He is accepting of Queequeg and of Queequeg's very different religious beliefs, finding much good, much decency in that which is initially strange to him. He also possesses a good sense of humor and a cheerful attitude, brushing away fears of death in Father Mapple's New Bedford chapel. He wants to learn, he wants to find out about the world, and he wants the *Pequod* to be his classroom. Knowing nothing of whaling, he is curious and wants to experience it. "I want to see what whaling is," he says. "I want to see the world."[29]

This attitude of openness extends also to his fellows on board. They, too, are separate Selves, autonomous, liberal entities — but they are *not* searching. They all think they know how to relate to Other. "They were nearly all Islanders in the *Pequod*," he says. "Isolatoes too, I call such, not acknowledging the common continent of men, but each Isolato living on a separate continent of his own."[30] Ishmael tries to establish linkages with them, however, although most of the connectives are fleeting and symbolically illusory, as is the case in "A Squeeze of the Hand." Only with Queequeg (perhaps the most Other of them all), does Ishmael establish a deeper, more significant relationship — one based on mutual respect, affection and understanding. At first patronizing towards Queequeg, Ishmael comes to see him as fundamentally decent and fundamentally worthy of respect in his own right.

Of course, Ishmael will be rewarded for this acceptance of the integrity of Other by being rescued by Queequeg's coffin at the end. Thus, in effect, Melville is suggesting that the Self can only be saved from the self-destruction that befell Ahab and from the self-destruction that Ishmael was contemplating before going to sea, by profound, transcendent effort. One must see beyond the ideological box of one's society and establish a proper, balanced, respectful relationship to Other.

Thus the entire voyage is, for Ishmael, a lesson in which he comes to experience this very consanguinity. Starting off cheerful, optimistic and confident in his basic attitude towards the world, although gnawed by a vague and serious discontent, he comes to intuitively realize that all personal *weltanschauungs* are fundamentally flawed. After his experience in "The Mast-Head," after his misperception of the real world, he realizes how frightening and dangerous the beautiful sea can be, how the "most dreaded creatures" are "treacherously hidden beneath the loveliest tints of azure."[31] He also comes to understand, contrariwise, how good, how benevolent, initially frightening things can be — as in the case of Queequeg. He realizes how brief, but cherished, are our moments of connectiveness with Other, or others, and how we therefore yearn for more than our individualist isolation. He sees, at the end, how all the different self-confident philosophies of Ahab, Starbuck, Stubb, Flask, Fedallah and the others availed them nought when Moby-Dick destroyed the ship. He becomes aware that "experience is composed of gratuitous events and disconnected sensations without significance or direction. This disturbing truth, which makes an orderly life impossible, usually remains hidden behind the many forms which man imposes on the world, since he convinces himself that they are inherent in the nature of experience itself." But Ishmael learns that "Whatever seems stable in experience has been put there by (man) himself. The hierarchical social structure aboard a well-ordered ship, the constructs of science and pseudo-science, pagan and Christian religious systems, even the concepts of space and time —

all of the forms which man uses to assure himself that everything which happens follows certain laws — are revealed . . . as passing fables."[32]

All man's presumed knowledge of the non-Self is, then, just folly. All the grand, interpretive schemata are mere distortions of Other by Self. Man knows nothing of the noumenal reality of Other and, besides, his questing to know is potentially dangerous. He may ask questions, as does Ishmael, but if he accepts any answers as real, as do Ahab and the others, only destruction will follow.

We must, though, continue to ask questions, without assuming we will find answers, for then we are saved, like Ishmael. By questing, Ishmael realized a deeper understanding of his aloneness in the universe. In the beginning, his alienation was palpable and deeply felt, but it was not comprehended in its full metaphysical dimensions. He thought his feelings were unnatural and he tried to escape them. It is only through the process of the voyage that he comes to see that the aloneness he experienced is truly endemic to the Self, that there is no way that Self and Other can become one, that there is no transcendentalist, pantheistic or Christian answer to the Self's apartness.

His adopted "desperado philosophy," as he terms it, allows him, then, an essential proportional balance between Self and Other. His intense particularity, his intense Self-ness, is balanced by the depth, the unknowability, of Other. He says that he has "doubts of all things earthly, and intuitions of some things heavenly; this combination makes neither believer nor infidel," he concludes, "but makes a man who regards them both with equal eye."[33] He learns that both Self and Other are on an equal plane, but that Self yearns for Other, that Other is unreachable and that the failure of the quest must be accepted by the Self. He realizes, too, that Self must try to find what satisfaction it can in the "little things" of life. Ishmael comes to appreciate that man must "eventually lower, or at least shift, his conceit of attainable felicity; not placing it anywhere in the intellect or the fancy; but in the wife, the heart, the bed, the table, the saddle, the fire-side, the country."[34]

IV

In the end, the real, grand quest ends with this. Ishmael is saved only because he comes to realize that the universe (or the ocean or

Moby-Dick), is ultimately unfathomable. He is redeemed because, "inured to loneliness and loss,"[35] he accepts the isolated liberal Self in its deepest dimension, in its balance with inscrutable Other. He throws Locke overboard, and Kant too, warning that the former will tilt you to one side and the latter will weigh you down.[36]

Modern liberal, existential man has thus turned out to be profoundly deeper and far more complex than either Locke's or Kant's early liberal man. The Self's autonomy, the Self's aloneness, is far more intense, far deeper than either imagined. We are, in the end, more than just individuals, we are orphans, cast out by our biblical father. We are like Ishmael, who, in the conclusion, is saved only "by another loser, by the now childless captain of the Rachel, whose own beloved sons have been lost. The old order is past, but perhaps a new one will come; perhaps a new relationship can take the place of the old familial one, one which will begin, perhaps, with the recognition that all men are now orphans."[37]

Only thus, Melville suggests, if we see ourselves as fellow cosmic isolatoes, without any of our gods, can we be saved. Perhaps this connective in an empty universe, this monkey-rope on a sliding whale,[38] can preserve us against the "sharkish" nature of the world, of Hobbesian, American society. Perhaps this indirect linkage, this "squeeze of the hand," would be of greater value than all the false unities that are usually offered to us. In sharkish American society, the society from which Ishmael fled, this could be the only connective that is really viable, for America is so peopled by Hobbesian, rapacious isolatoes, as Melville knew. Only if we all go on Ishmael's metaphysical, mythic journey can we preserve, perhaps, our Selves and our society, at all. The alternative could be wreckage, destruction, the victory of brute disorder — Ahab's fate. And the sea will roll on as it did five thousand years ago, in the beginning.

What Melville appears to propose, then, is nothing less than a radical intensification of liberalism, to the point where liberal Selves realize their common aloneness in the universe. Thus will our short-term differences pale beside our existential commonality. Our sharkish appetites can perhaps be restrained in no other way. Liberal government cannot do it, as Melville makes clear in "Stubb's Supper," and neither can religion. "No use a-preaching to such dam g'uttons" for "dey don't hear one word" says Fleece.[39] Only a common consciousness of how we are all isolated shipmates, all orphans, can save us.

Yet Melville remains ambiguous about the practical reality of this possibility, for, after all, only one soul was saved on the *Pequod* and a great disaster, in the end, did occur. Ishmael survived "as the voyaging mind, the capacity for vision, the potentiality of symbolic perception,"[40] but this is a mixed blessing, for the next voyage could just as easily be that of another Ahab as of an Ishmael. We are left then with a "double attitude in Melville — an acceptance of 'voyaging' and a fear of its full implications."[41] We cannot be sure, then, that Melville is at all hopeful for liberal man.

But still, Ishmael, surely a liberal Self *par excellence*, does survive, so Melville seems to imply that some, at least, can have a proper Self-Other relationship, even though these few cannot save the ship, cannot save the larger human society from destruction or even from sharkishness. As long as an Ishmael, an Everyman, survives, however, the hope can persist. American liberal man just might, in the end, collectively find his deeper, existential Self and preserve his sociopolitical, interpretive order.

Notes

1. Howard P. Vincent, *The Trying-out of Moby-Dick* (Kent, Ohio: Kent State University Press, 1949), 45.
2. John Locke, *Essay Concerning Human Understanding*, ed. Peter H. Nidditch (Oxford: Clarendon Press, 1979).
3. David Hume, *A Treatise of Human Nature*, ed. C.A. Selby-Bigge (Oxford: Clarendon Press, 1888).
4. Immanuel Kant, *The Critique of Pure Reason*, trans. N.K. Smith (New York: St. Martin's Press, 1929).
5. Herman Melville, *Moby-Dick* (London, Collins, 1977), 145.
6. Ibid., 478.
7. See, for example, Ahab's great speech in Melville, "The Quarter Deck," chap. 36 in *Moby-Dick*.
8. See, for example, Ahab's rejection of the real business of the voyage in Melville, "Ahab and Starbuck in the Cabin," chap. 109 in *Moby-Dick*. He is not interested in making money. He is interested in slaying Moby-Dick.
9. See, Joseph C. Bertolini, "The Existential Paradox and Political Theory" (Ph.D. diss., New York University, 1983), Chapter 3.
10. Richard B. Sewall, *The Vision of Tragedy* (New Haven: Yale U. Press, 1980),102.
11. Melville, *Moby-Dick,* 166.
12. Ibid., 149.
13. Ibid.
14. Ibid., 477.
15. Tyrus Hillway, *Herman Melville* (Boston: Twayne, 1963), 90.
16. Vincent, *The Trying-out of Moby-Dick*, 179.
17. Ibid., 179-180.
18. Hillway, *Herman Melville,* 91.
19. This language is consciously Heideggerrian. Much of Heidegger's thought would seem to be related to Melville's conception of the Self-Other relationship. See, for example, Martin Heidegger, *Begin and Nothingness,* trans. Hazel E. Barnes (New York: Philosophical Library, 1956); and George Steiner, *Martin Heidegger* (New York: Viking, 1978).
20. Melville, *Moby-Dick*, 145.
21. Ibid., 414.
22. Ibid., 366.
23. Ibid., 370.
24. Ibid., 325.
25. Henry Nash Smith, "The Image of Society in *Moby-Dick,*" in *Twentieth Century Interpretation of Moby-Dick,* ed. Michael T. Gilmore (Englewood Cliffs, N.J.: Prentice-Hall, 1977), 31.
26. Melville, *Moby-Dick*, 17.

27. Ibid., 19.
28. Ibid., 21.
29. Ibid., 74.
30. Ibid., 113.
31. Ibid., 242.
32. Edgar A. Dryden, *Melville's Thematics of Form:The Great Art of Telling the Truth* (Baltimore: The Johns Hopkins Press, 1968), 83.
33. Melville, *Moby-Dick*, 321.
34. Ibid., 356.
35. Pearl Chester Solomon, *Dickens and Melville in Their Time* (New York: Columbia University Press, 1975), 4.
36. See Melville, "Stubb and Flask Kill a Right Whale; and Then Have a Talk Over Him," chap. 73 in *Moby-Dick*.
37. Solomon, *Dickens and Melville in Their Time*, 4.
38. See Melville, "The Monkey-Rope," chap. 72 in *Moby-Dick*.
39. Ibid., 258.
40. Charles Feidelson, Jr., "Symbolism in *Moby-Dick*," in *Critics on Melville,* ed. Thomas J. Rountree (Coral Gables, Florida: University of Miami Press, 1972), 84.
41. Ibid., 85.

Chapter 5

Huckleberry Finn

I

In *Huckleberry Finn*, as in *The Scarlet Letter* and *Moby-Dick*, one can find a fundamental Lockean, individualist ethic with darker Hobbesian, wholly self-regarding, aggressive elements and also a contradictory Protestant liberal conscience.[1]

To make this argument, however, is, of course, not to suggest that there is only one possible interpretation of Twain's book. There have been many meanings assigned to the text[2] but, from the standpoint of political theory, the argument proffered here is essentially to be regarded as a variation on America's consistent Lockean liberal theme, America's intersubjectively shared consciousness. *Huckleberry Finn*, that is, is to be understood as another example of the cultural viscosity of the elemental, liberal formation of consciousness that constitutes the American sociopolitical culture.[3]

Actually, the idea of the highly individuated, liberal self has long been accepted as a hallmark of American fictive literature. The

American fictional hero has been referred to as "the American Adam," as "an individual emancipated from history, happily bereft of ancestry untouched and undefiled by the usual inheritances of family and race; an individual standing alone, self-reliant and self-propelling, ready to confront whatever awaited him with the aid of his own unique and inherent resources."[4] This is American man as an "Emersonian figure, 'the simple genuine self against the whole world.' "[5] It is a theme that resonated in the nation's fiction virtually from its inception right through to the present. Saul Bellow's contemporary characters, for example, readily recall "the slippery heroism of *Huckleberry Finn*."[6]

American Adamic man as a decent innocent refers to the Lockean side of the American individual while Adam, regarded as a sinner, refers to a darker, more Hobbesian dimension of the American self. Both aspects of the American individual are found in *Huckleberry Finn*.

Further, Huck's intensification of his individualism can be thought of as a type of pre-existentialist experience in which, as a very isolated Self, cut off from "normal" society, he develops a more balanced metaphysical relationship with Other, which, in this case, is represented by Jim. Potentially, though, all Americans, compelled culturally to be Hobbesian-Lockean isolatoes, can develop the same existential depth, which could link them with the tragic vision as well. In this sense, Huck is a prototype for a form of liberalism with potential transcendent capacity.

II

More basically, though, Huck Finn should be thought of as the quintessential rebel, an essential ingredient for the later development of existential intensity. Huck's "profoundly anti-social values"[7] are clearly and brazenly exhibited earlier in *Tom Sawyer* and throughout *Huckleberry Finn*. Huck refuses to be "sivilized" by the Widow Douglas. He says that "It was rough living in the house all the time, considering how dismal regular and decent the widow was in all her ways; and so when I couldn't stand it no longer I lit out. I got into my old rags and my sugar hogshead again, and was free and satisfied."[8] The widow tries to teach him Biblical stories but he "don't take no stock in dead people," so he pays no real attention to them. He is also acutely aware of social hypocrisy, finding no sense in the widow's criticism of his smoking habit while she casually takes snuff. Huck complains that "it got tiresome and lonesome" because Miss Watson, the widow's sister, "kept pecking at me." He "felt so lonesome (he) most wished (he) was dead."[9]

Huck, then, is uncomfortable with rules, structures and institutions. They clearly make him feel alienated. He is only content, only at one with himself, when he is "simple and free," when he is Walt Whitman's "natural man."[10] Clothes are oppressive, homes are oppressive, and table manners are oppressive. When he gets away from these things, he can be himself. He is, in short, autonomous man, content and essentially self-sufficient unto himself, although, of course, being human, he does need to reach out to others, as he does to Jim and other characters in the novel. He always remains separate from his surroundings, however, always critical, self-reliant and essentially self-fulfilling. He is never lonely when he is alone, for example. He is only lonely when he is *in* conventional society, when he is in a situation that requires senseless, oppressive subordination. He is not lonely with Jim on the raft or with the Grangerfords because in these situations he is regarded and related to with the respect due to any autonomous self. On the raft, with Jim, Huck comes to realize that Jim is his *friend*, not just a faithful dog, as Southern society would perceive him, and that Jim is, therefore, really another autonomous self, ultimately as much of an isolato, as he is. He learns to respect Jim, respect his feelings, and care for him. And he realizes that, although he is a black slave, Jim is just like himself — another autonomous entity with needs and inner complexities.

The relationship they enter into, then, is the ideal one between Lockean individuated selves. They create their own little world, based on mutual respect for each other's otherness. Neither one ultimately uses or exploits the other. Their needs for autonomy and genuine relatedness are at least temporarily realized. As Huck says, "There warn't no home like a raft, after all. Other places do seem so cramped up and smothery, but a raft don't. You feel mighty free and easy and comfortable on a raft."[11]

Further, they come together and stay together out of a mutual need to protect themselves against the savageries of the world about them. The surrounding shores are lined with people who engage in the cruelest, stupidest and most appalling behavior. They journey through a horrendously dangerous place from which they are in constant danger of attack. In the end, they are shot at by relatives and they are often in situations where death is a real possibility. So they cut away and create their Lockean island literally in the middle of all the cruelty and insanity. And, since nearly everyone they encounter is violent and cruel in one way or another, it is clear that while the raft is Lockean in nature, the world about them is, in essence, rapaciously Hobbesian.

Of course, Huck and Jim are obviously not conscious of any philosophical, Hobbesian-Lockean distinction between their floating world and what is occurring on shore. They naturally cannot perceive the conceptual import of the raft, but they nonetheless create a different world anyway, establishing a kinder, gentler, Lockean version of the Hobbesian individualism around them. If Hartz is right and Locke is in our cultural DNA, then we should not be surprised that this would happen. Nor should we be surprised that the Hobbesian underside of Locke should be everywhere around the raft.

Both realities are clearly experienced by Huck, the book's narrator. He tells again and again of the self-aggrandizing and violent people he meets on the Hobbesian shore but his experience with Jim is also real to him and it is his awareness of the reality of this positive, respectful relationship that ultimately leads to his great moral moment — his refusal to turn Jim in. "It is the memory of Jim's kindness and goodness . . . that impels Huck to defy his conscience"[12] — a conscience that is only really *his* when, on the raft, he is "clear of the perverted value system of St. Petersburg."[13] On the raft, in the Lockean world created in a primal state of nature, Huck, when thinking about what to do about Jim, "is now quite alone."[14] The debate in his head concerning Jim "is not affected by any stimulus from the outside."[15] He is governed now by the self-created Lockean rules of respect and mutually regarded self-interest. They develop naturally when one can cut away from the darker, Hobbesian individualism and twisted southern feudalism that permeates society.

In fact, Huck's individualism is so intensified on the raft and so radically deepened that he becomes more than just a rebel against society — he becomes a rebel against God. When he says that he will "give up sin," be a good boy and turn Jim in, he knows he is just "playing double." He says,

> I was letting on to give up sin but away inside of me I was holding on to the biggest one of all. I was trying to make my mouth say I would do the right thing and the clean thing . . . and tell where he was: but deep down in me I knowed it was a lie, and He knowed it. You can't pray a lie — I found that out.[16]

Clearly,

The important psychological discovery in the passage involves the equivalence of God's knowledge and Huck's knowledge. Huck certainly contains severe conflict, but there is no conventional self-abasement, no commitment of self to God no matter what, no attitude of *in manuas tuas*. Instead, we see Huck's realization that it does no good to hide the truth *from himself either*. That basic perception, that self is equal to God in insight and importance, forms the core of Huck's morality. This respect for individual conscience contributes to the novel's appeal to our culture.[17]

But the world Huck and Jim have created, for all of its value to their integrity and individuation, cannot last. It is an anomaly, an anachronism really. In fact, the rather silly, bizarre ending to the story is due to Twain's realization that Huck's and Jim's world, their quest, could not succeed. He had "to admit finally to himself that Huck's and Jim's journey down the river could not be imagined as leading to freedom for either of them."[18] Earlier, "Twain had shattered the raft under the paddle wheel of a steamboat. He now destroy(ed) it again, symbolically, by revealing that Huck's and Jim's journey, with all its anxieties (had) been pointless."[19] The fact that Miss Watson, as Tom Sawyer reveals, had already freed Jim in her will had made the whole enterprise presumably unnecessary.

There had thus been something clearly unreal about the venture, but, more to the point, there had been something unreal about a Lockean island in a Hobbesian world. The raft, after all, is swamped by the forces of selfish brutality. America, then, Twain would seem to be saying, may very well be Lockean at its best, but its overwhelming expression of individualism is much more Hobbesian.

III

Twain believes that human nature is fundamentally selfish. The best we can do, he writes, is to advance from "unreasoned selfishness to reasoned selfishness. All our acts, reasoned and unreasoned, are selfish."[20] Hence we do terrible things to each other, simply because we are basically self-centered and not essentially empathetic beings. "Human beings can be awful cruel to one another"[21] as Huck says. And the cruelties are not *perceived* as cruelties by the average individual in a given culture because everyone else around him is acting the same way. Given cultures, that is, *sanction* certain cruelties and outlaw others. The Grangerfords, for example, are supposed to be models of Southern civility — at least Huck thinks so. Huck remarks that "Colonel Grangerford was a gentleman . . . a gentleman all over; and so was his family. . . . He was as kind as could be."[22] Exercising all the sensitive virtues of traditional Southern hospitality, he treated Huck impeccably well. But Twain sees him as a parody of what a real gentleman would be. After all, Grangerford kept slaves and slaughtered Shepherdsons whenever he could get his hands on them.

Huck himself is no angel. He is hardly any sort of noble savage. There is certainly nothing Rousseauian, therefore, about Twain's thought — nothing really radical, nothing to the left, in his critique. There is no reason to believe that Twain intended *Huckleberry Finn* "to become a general indictment of civilization in favor of primitivism or the frontier."[23] To make this case is to ignore Pap. "Pap was a real rogue. . . . He was a thief and a drunk, illiterate, filthy, full of howling hate against blacks, schools, cleanliness, and respectability, a con artist and a sadist. . . . Pap was a man with nothing to show for the frontier experience but the experience of cultural erosion."[24] So much, then, for Rousseau — and for Turner[25] as well.

Of course, Pap is not the best refutation of Rousseau's "noble savage" idea. In fact, for Twain, he is really a caricature of the concept. He is, roughly, a man of the frontier but he is not wholly outside of society. Actually, he is on its bottommost rung. Nonetheless, Twain seems to be saying that man is not so filled with natural goodness that *just* detaching from society or *just* being on the frontier will foster virtue and decency. For the latter to be realized, one has to regard one's apartness as the opportunity for intense self-inquiry, as Huck does.

Certainly, Huck, the "natural man," "borrows" and lies with casual ease and judges what is moral or immoral on the basis of how he feels afterwards about what he did. There is more Benthamism than Rousseauian radicalism in him. He is only saved, he is only redeemed, because he engages in autonomous self-examination.

Similarly, Huck does not achieve salvation "by merely paying lip service to the dogmas or rituals of organized religion"[26] or to feudal values. The novel, that is, is not a rightist critique either. Huck describes how, for example, the Grangerfords and the Shepherdsons, those "noble" southerners, go to church *together* and listen to sermons about brotherly love "and such-like tiresomeness" and then, at home, talk all about "faith and good works and free grace and pre-foreordestination."[27] Then, a few days later, they murder each other. Orthodoxy cannot be the answer for American liberal, individualist man.

Huck, thus, moves neither left nor right to rise above the Hobbesian madness around him. Instead, he goes into himself in a reflexive manner made possible by his separation from the rote cultural programming from which he has escaped. He relies on his own innate common sense, his careful analysis of experience, his skeptical and critical mind and his willingness to trust his sincere feelings for others. When he *does* treat well those he cares about, he *feels* better about it and he knows then that he is right. He knows intuitively that the self, at its best, must try to connect with other autonomous selves and that, by doing so, one does what one needs for at least partial self-realization. This is the Protestant American impulse at its best, the attainment of certain individualist goals via the application of the "golden rule." Of course, the "golden rule" would naturally come into contradiction with *purely* self-aggrandizing goals.

Thus, Huck's method of relating to his surroundings is crucial to his Lockean individualism. Twain's style here is very important. After all, it has been generally agreed that of all "our great prose writers . . . he is the 'most American.'"[28] He demonstrates this by having Huck describe his reality in a manner well befitting any Lockean liberal. It is, in fact,

> Huck's attention to empirical detail that gives his observations such colour and immediacy. His words do not deny things as they are, they acknowledge them and derive their beauty from the acknowledgement; his eloquence depends on patient observation, in fact, a fierce sense of the particular. And it is even more apparent, perhaps, from Huck's judgments and actions. For, like many subsequent American heroes, Huck is easily the most honourable and, indeed, chivalric character in his world simply because he sticks closest to the facts. To be more precise, it is Huck's realistic awareness of other people and objects, his understanding of their separateness and individuality that allows him to assume, without being priggish, a certain nobility; he sees Jim as someone in his own right, commanding respect and requiring sympathy. . . . [29]

For example, when Huck is trying to decide whether he should turn Jim in or not, he says he

> got to thinking over our trip down the river; and I see Jim before me all the time: in the day and in the nighttime, sometimes moonlight, sometimes storms, and we a-floating along, talking and singing and laughing. But somehow I couldn't seem to strike no places to harden me against him, but only the other kind. I'd see him standing my watch on top of his'n, 'stead of calling me, so I could go on sleeping; and see him how glad he was when I come back out of the fog; and when I come to him again in the swamp, up there where the feud was; and such-like times; and would always call me honey, and pet me, and do everything he could think of for me, and how good he always was; and at last I struck the time I saved him by telling the men we had smallpox aboard, and he was so grateful, and said I was the best friend old Jim ever had in the world, and the *only* one he's got now.[30]

These experiences, these events, stand for themselves in Huck's mind. He *knows* these events occurred and he *knows* how he felt about them. That is all he needs.

No wonder Hemingway admired *Huckleberry Finn* so much. Twain (and the first World War) had taught him to see the world in terms of separate entities only.

Huck, therefore, the autonomous self, sees others as autonomous selves also and he sees events in their discrete particularity. He sees the world, that is, through liberal, empiricist lenses. All of the others in the novel *interpret* facts through some imposed ideology, including Jim, Tom Sawyer, Sherburn etc. By their so doing, people and events are sacrificed to imaginative interpretation and immense cruelties are performed because they fail to see people as isolated autonomous selves, i.e. they fail to see others as being autonomous entities like themselves. In this regard, northern capitalist ideology can be just as distorting as southern semi-feudal ideology.

Of course, Huck, too, *initially* perceives the world through the southern semi-feudal gestalt. It is only because he breaks with that culture and then becomes introspective on the raft that he begins to appreciate reality as a discrete, Lockean individualist.

IV

Twain here would seem to be suggesting that the way out of the Hobbesian war of all against all could be a full acceptance of the real implications of our autonomous individualism, i.e. he would be for an enlightened self-interest, a form of Kantian morality. This principle could have been applied both to the old South, which for so long was twisted by a peculiar variant of feudal thinking, by "Sir Walter Scottism," as to the industrial North, which had sacrificed enlightened individualism for an all-encompassing capitalist mentality.[31] Twain, actually, would have preferred a return to a sort of Jeffersonian Arcadia, as he described it, after the Civil War. This is what he tries to have Huck and Jim realize on the raft. He wants them to experience an idyllic, imagined Jeffersonian world in which autonomous citizens respect both themselves and each other. However, just as the raft is doomed, Twain comes to believe that this hope is doomed as well. He becomes more and more disillusioned and pessimistic as he sees the ostensibly liberating forces of technology and industrialization create new evils for Americans. He realizes that simplicity, naturalness and lucidity, the virtues that will make our Lockean world work properly and virtuously, are being overwhelmed by new "isms" and "ologies," using Dickens' oft mentioned terms.

As Twain saw it, we were still, after the Civil War, unable to see clearly; unable to be autonomous selves at our best. We continued to live in seemingly perpetual cultural fantasies. The Civil War had just replaced one false perspective with another.

Given Mark Twain's philosophy, it is not surprising that he will come to this conclusion. He is, of course, a man of great complexity and, to a degree, a "man of contradictions,"[32] but there is a clear thread in his thought that leads us directly to *Huckleberry Finn*. In *What is Man?*, "the only extended and disciplined effort he ever made to pierce to the roots of man's nature,"[33] he clearly reveals his liberal individualism. He argues that "the sole impulse that ever moves a person to do a thing" is "to content his own spirit,"[34] that "there is *no* act large or small, fine or mean, which springs from any motive"[35] but that one, that "love, hate, charity, compassion, avarice, benevolence and so on . . . are all forms of self-contentment, self gratification."[36]

This is standard Hobbesian-Lockean thinking in that it establishes the autonomous individual as the inevitable center of all purpose. Further, Twain holds that man "gets *all* his ideas, all his impressions, from the outside,"[37] denying that man is naturally inclined to good.

Therefore, training and temperament are everything. Within the limits of one's natural disposition, the one you are born with, you can be trained "upward and still upward toward a summit where you will find your chiefest pleasure in conduct which, while contenting you, will be sure to confer benefits on your neighbor and the community."[38] Thus, Twain believes that man is "merely a machine,"[39] (a very Hobbesian idea) and he *can* be made better. He *can* be made into a decent citizen, who learns to serve himself by serving others. But Twain does not have much hope for this. He knows men have a tendency to accept as valid whatever overarching truth they are initially exposed to or find to be congenial. "He (knows) the impenetrable stubbornness of ideas fixed in childhood and sanctified by the halo of public approval."[40] As such, social training does not serve man's real betterment, does not teach true, other-regarding virtues, but, instead, is devoted to some cultural or ideological half-truth.[41] This pessimism is fully expressed in *The Mysterious Stranger* and *A Connecticut Yankee in King Arthur's Court*.

Twain, then, forces us "to examine the fears and hatreds that lie beneath the veneer of civilized habits and customs."[42] And what lay underneath is pure egotism. Twain believes that "Nothing runs deeper in man's nature than the necessity for self-preservation"[43] and that "Before the drive of self-preservation, ideals fall shattered and helpless."[44] The Enlightenment is but a thin gilding covering a deep Hobbesian-Lockean drive of self-interest, pursued at any cost, but often papered over with respectability. Man's capacity for lying, Twain holds, is limitless and state and society impose whatever circumscribed and distorted values are necessary for their continued existence.

In this type of situation, all that the sane person can do is to flee, to move on to where he can be true to *himself* at least, if he can. Actually, this is a classical American response to problem solving. And, at the end of *Huckleberry Finn*, Huck does exactly this, saying in the book's last lines, "Got to light out for the territory ahead of the rest, because Aunt Sally she's going to adopt me and sivilize me, and I can't stand it. I been there before."[45]

In the end, Twain seems to believe that one must either conform to some arbitrary interpretation of reality or stick to the facts, be really a Lockean autonomous Self and continually strike out anew, on your own. To be true to yourself you must flee any order, any community, that is not existentially self-generated. This is a harsh prescription, but perhaps the only salvational one for liberal man — and it is all given literary expression in *Huckleberry Finn*.

But, still, nothing can detract from Huck's great moment of Lockean individualist assertiveness when, in the climactic moral moment in the book, he refuses to turn Jim in. He does this even though he believes, as he had been taught by southern society, that to help a slave escape was a sin, a sin that would result in his being sent to hell. "All right, I'll go to hell,"[46] Huck says, but he will not harm his friend, another Self that Huck has come to see as an individuated entity like himself, with needs and feelings.

This act, with its application of the "golden rule," is a clear example of Huck's Lockean Protestant individualism, just as his sometimes more negative behavior is indicative of his more self-aggrandizing side. The latter also exemplifies Huck's Hobbesian dimension. Hobbesian behavior, of course, is found throughout the novel in the actions of the Duke, the Dauphin and so many other characters.

V

Twain's *Huckleberry Finn*, therefore, is a great American novel because it addresses the key concept of American sociopolitical culture, liberal individualism, in all of its complexity and with its several dimensions. Hobbesian-Lockean individualism is not only present in the work but is really what the novel is all about. The novel makes clear that we live now in a shallow, violent, more and more Hobbesian world, as Twain sees it, but that we can also use the heart of our American liberal ethic to envision our world differently. We see the possibility that intense existential apartness can generate a viable need for a connective with Other which can have real transcendent intensity.

Twain, after all, always tempers his pessimism with his enjoyment of the very experience of being alive. In this he is similar to Camus. If life, in its potential, is so good, but often turns out so bad because of man's self-centeredness, isn't there still the chance that there may be moments of real decency? If man is a complex, deterministic machine, may not the mix get so occasionally juggled that someone may achieve real virtue? Perhaps even a whole society can do this. Twain, though, in his later years, thought that this was not likely. So we come back to the heroic individual — to Huck's great moral moment.

Huckleberry Finn, then, in conclusion, makes the case for America as a Lockean liberal society but it also goes beyond this to describe a darker America that can be redeemed only by the most lucid, intense, personal self-examination — the kind of introspection one can engage in far from the madding, Hobbesian crowd while on a raft on the big river.

Notes

1. An earlier version of this chapter appeared as an article in *The Michigan Academician*. See Joseph C. Bertolini, "Locke on a Raft: Twain's *Huckleberry Finn* and the Hartzian Thesis Expanded," 26, no.3 (Summer, 1994):449-461.
2. See, for example, James M. Cox, "Remarks on the Sad Initiation of Huckleberry Finn," *Sewanee Review* 62(Summer, 1954): 389-405; Kenneth Lynn, "Huck and Jim," *Yale Review* 47 (1958): 421-431; Arnold Rampersad, "*Adventures of Huckleberry Finn* and Afro-American Literature," *Mark Twain Journal* 22, no. 2 (1984): 47-52; Forrest G. Robinson, *In Bad Faith: The Dynamics of Deception in Mark Twain's America* (Cambridge, Massachusetts: Harvard U. Press, 1986); and Sherwood Cummings, *Mark Twain and Science* (Baton Rouge: Louisiana State University Press, 1988).
3. H. Mark Roelofs, *Ideology and Myth in American Politics* (Boston: Little, Brown, 1976), 32.
4. R. W. B. Lewis, *The American Adam* (Chicago: University of Chicago Press, 1955), 5.
5. Ibid.,198.
6. Ibid.
7. Richard Gray, "Kingdom and Exile: Mark Twain's Hannibal Books," in *American Fiction: New Readings* (Totowa, New Jersey: Vision, 1983), 87.
8. Mark Twain, *The Adventures of Huckleberry Finn* (New York: New American Library, 1959),11.
9. Ibid.,13.
10. Gladys Carmen Bellamy, "Roads to Freedom," in *Twentieth Century Interpretations of The Adventures of Huckleberry Finn,* ed. Claude Simpson (Englewood Cliffs, New Jersey: Prentice-Hall, 1968), 17.
11. Twain, *Huckleberry Finn*, 119.
12. Henry Nash Smith, *Mark Twain: The Development of a Writer* (Cambridge, Mass.: Harvard University Press, 1962),121.
13. Ibid.,120.
14. Ibid.
15. Ibid., 121.
16. Twain, *Huckleberry Finn*, 209.
17. Victor A. Doyno, *Writing Huck Finn* (Philadelphia: University of Pennsylvania Press, 1991), 155.
18. Henry Nash Smith, *Mark Twain*, 132.
19. Ibid., 133.
20. Quoted in Walter Blair, "So Noble . . . and So Beautiful a Book," in *Twentieth Century Interpretations of Huckleberry Finn*, ed. Claude Simpson(Englewood Cliffs, New Jersey: Prentice-Hall, 1968), 65.

21. Twain, *Huckleberry Finn*, 225.
22. Ibid.,108.
23. Edwin H. Cady, *The Light of Common Day* (Bloomington, Indiana: Indiana University Press, 1971), 104.
24. Ibid.
25. Frederick Jackson Turner, *The Frontier in American History* (New York: Holt, 1920).
26. Gilbert M. Rubenstein, "The Moral Structure of *Huckleberry Finn*," in *Twentieth Century Interpretations of The Adventures of Huckleberry Finn*, ed. Claude Simpson (Englewood Cliffs, New Jersey: Prentice-Hall, 1968), 59.
27. Twain, *Huckleberry Finn*, 112.
28. Richard Chase, *The American Novel and its Tradition* (Garden City, New York: Doubleday, 1957), 150.
29. Gray, "Kingdom and Exile," 90-91.
30. Twain, *Huckleberry Finn*, 209-210.
31. See Mark Twain, *The Gilded Age* (with C.D. Warner), (Hartford: American Publishing Co., 1873).
32. Richard Hofstadter, *Anti-intellectualism in American Life* (New York: Knopf, 1970), 242.
33. Don M. Wolfe, *The Image of Man in America* (New York: Thomas Y. Crowell, 1957), 200.
34. Mark Twain, *What is Man?* (New York: Harper, 1917), 12.
35. Ibid., 19.
36. Ibid., 28-29.
37. Ibid., 47.
38. Ibid., 54-55.
39. Ibid., 75.
40. Wolfe, *The Image of Man in America*, 218.
41. Twain, *What is Man?*, 74-75.
42. Wolfe, *The Image of Man in America*, 200.
43. Ibid., 203.
44. Ibid., 200.
45. Twain, *Huckleberry Finn*, 283.
46. Ibid., 210.

Chapter 6

ଽଠଓଽ

The Great Gatsby

I

Irving Howe, in his classic *Politics and the Novel*, argues perceptively that "One of the most striking facts about American life and literature is the frequency with which political issues seem to arise in non-political forms. Instead of confronting us as formidable systems of thought, or as parties locked in bitter combat, politics in America has often appeared in the guise of religious, cultural and sexual issues. . . . "[1]

Thus, "In those nineteenth century American novels that do deal with politics, ideology or what passes for it in this country, is seen in a far more intimate relation to personal experience than in the European political novel; in fact ideology is sometimes treated by the American novelists as if it were merely a form of private experience. . . . "[2] Reducing everything to Self, American novelists naturally "could not quite do justice to the life of politics in its own right (but) personalizing everything, they could brilliantly observe how social and individual experience melt into one another so that the deformations of one soon became the deformations of the other."[3] And, according to Howe, what one derives from these American novels that at once obliquely and profoundly touch upon politics is an image of isolation, "an isolation that a wounded intelligence is trying desperately to transform into the composure of solitude."[4]

Howe's acute analysis, relevant, of course, in terms of the three previous novels, is particularly applicable to *The Great Gatsby*. This story of one man's pursuit of an idealized American dream is really a personalized version of American liberal culture. Gatsby unconsciously plays out the down side of the American, Hobbesian-Lockean ideology and thereby relates his life to a philosophical foundation, but, like most Americans, is never aware that he is doing so.

II

The Great Gatsby is, of course, F. Scott Fitzgerald's finest work and, arguably, a candidate for the "Great American Novel." The novel is not only a description of fragmented, individuated man in America but also a form of jeremiad, a moral denouncing of this situation.[5] It makes a strong case for America as a land of highly fragmented, alienated and self-absorbed individuals seeking to attain happiness. In effect, Fitzgerald gives us a version of T. S. Eliot's "The Wasteland." Fitzgerald admired Eliot and very much had "The Wasteland" in mind when he wrote *Gatsby*. His vision of America and Eliot's vision of modernity closely parallel each other. They both saw fragmentation, alienation and spiritual emptiness all around them.

Gatsby, however, with its particular American focus, clearly describes a society without any social bondedness. In the New York of the novel, people pursue separate materialist ambitions, each in his or her own world. Other people are used and discarded, relationships either fail or lack all depth and purposeless, disconnected behavior is the norm. People are referred to as "worn-out men,"[6] more concerned with gesture than with substance and locked in their own worlds. Human interaction is reduced to "casual innuendo and introductions forgotten on the spot" and "enthusiastic meetings" between people who "never knew each other's names."[7] The principal character, Jay Gatsby, the impressive self-made man, is referred to as being in "complete isolation"[8] and "content to be alone"[9] while the narrator, Nick Carraway, is clearly conscious of his loneliness. Aloneness and apartness are everywhere. As Nick states, "At the enchanted metropolitan twilight

I felt a haunting loneliness sometimes, and felt it in others — poor young clerks who loitered in front of windows waiting until it was time for a solitary restaurant dinner — young clerks in the dusk, wasting the most poignant moments of night and life."[10] People are "incurably dishonest,"[11] deal in subterfuges,"[12] and go to large parties because "at small parties there isn't any privacy."[13] At these parties women have fights "with men *said* to be their husbands."[14] So the conjugal bond, to the extent that it exists in anything but name, is no haven and relationships, in general, are tenuous, chaotic and confused.

In such vacuity, people are cut off not only from each other but from any ordered set of values. Each is just buffeted about and attracted to or repelled by this or that interest or object in an apparently Hobbesian, mechanistic manner. Nothing seems to matter all that much. As Myrtle says, "I'm going to make a list of all the things I've got to get. A massage and a wave, and a collar for the dog, and one of those cute little ash trays where you touch a spring, and a wreath with a black silk bow for mother's grave that'll last all summer."[15] For Myrtle, a dog collar and a wreath for her mother's grave are items of equal priority. In "The Wasteland," there is nothing special about a mother-child relationship and no priority of values. Gatsby therefore clearly sees nothing wrong with Wolfsheim's fixing of the 1919 World Series and, in fact, sees nothing at all improper about his illegal attainment of wealth.

In such a world, where, as in "The Wasteland," "man's universe itself has cracked up,"[16] we all live in a "valley of ashes — a fantastic farm where ashes grow like wheat into ridges and hills and grotesque gardens; where ashes take the forms of houses and chimneys and rising smoke and, finally, with a transcendent effort, of ash-gray men who move dimly and already crumbling through the powdery air."[17]

Fitzgerald's description of a world that has become an ash-heap is an appropriate metaphor for a society with people who possess a "vicious emptiness,"[18] are "too empty" to have friends,[19] "don't belong to any" structure of transcendent purpose[20] and are "careless and confused," smashing up "things and creatures and then retreat(ing) back into their money or their vast carelessness, or whatever it was that kept them together."[21]

Virtue or ethical and religious values are no longer relevant — neither understood, appreciated nor remembered. God has been reduced to a forlorn billboard — the eyes of Dr. T. J. Eckleburg that, "dimmed . . . by many paintless days under sun and rain, brood on over the solemn dumping ground."[22] For Wilson, "God sees everything," but Michaelis reassures him that Dr. Eckleburg's eyes are just "an advertisement."[23] The self-restraint of Orthodoxy, generated by a fear of God, is long over. Now it is all just selfishness and money, according to Fitzgerald.

Unsurprisingly, "Fitzgerald seems at every point to emphasize the unconnectedness of Gatsby."[24] No one really seems to know who he is and he does not seem to know himself very well. Naive, really, about the world, he is naive about what he can attain. Having, in fact, made himself, having sprung "from his Platonic conception of himself,"[25] he is the ultimate, isolated, literally self-made, individualistic American — living in a world of essentially similar "isolatoes." Gatsby is no less a liberal, individuated self than those who attend his parties and people the rest of the novel. He differs from them only in that he still believes in the original myth of the American dream, i.e. "the naive dream based on the fallacious assumption that material possessions are synonymous with happiness, harmony and beauty."[26] He believes, like so many Americans, that the possession of material goods will bring spiritual satisfaction. Daisy, for him, is the symbol of this American dream. Her voice, after all, "is full of money — that was the inexhaustible charm that rose and fell in it, the jingle of it. . . ."[27] When he possesses her, he assumes, he will have achieved bliss — and money is the ticket to her acquisition. He is, in this respect, touchingly naive, but "He is truly great by virtue of his capacity to commit himself to his aspirations."[28]

Autonomous, then, and self-fulfilling and, ultimately, self-referential, Gatsby is Hobbesian-Lockean man living in a liberal society of individuated, materialist egos, living in a fragmented social order without any communal connectives. This is a society that is palpably more atomistic and materialistic than the earlier America of Hawthorne, Melville and Twain, so clearly there has been a steady, bourgeois intensification of the isolated Self as they would have imagined. And, although Gatsby represents an earlier, purer version of the American Self in his capacity for wonder, in the spiritual dimension of his self-fulfillment, this earlier version is no less liberal than what it develops into and, in fact, is similarly rent by its own conjoining of spiritual ends and materialist means into the Protestant/Bourgeois complex.

Gatsby, however, is not to be understood as a tragic hero in the sense that he clearly achieves self-understanding and lucid depth of vision before he is physically destroyed. He is not like Oedipus or

Lear. In Gatsby's case, all we have at the end is Nick's notion, his "idea," projected onto Gatsby, that "Gatsby himself didn't believe" any longer that Daisy would leave her husband for him and that perhaps Gatsby "no longer cared. If that were true, he must have looked up at an unfamiliar sky through frightening leaves and shivered as he found what a grotesque thing a rose is and how raw the sunlight was upon the scarcely created grass. A new world, material without being real. . . . "[29] In other words, he would have been even more starkly alone than before — he would now be self-created for only the Void. He would be even more of an isolato in a condition of complete natural and societal chaos, alone in a wholly material world unorganized by any imaginative imposition. He would have taken the Hobbesian-Lockean Self to the existentialist level. But since we have no evidence that Gatsby thought this way, we must presume that Nick's comment is really more indicative of his own propensity for tragic, existential awareness, a quality that he shares with no one else in the novel.

However, while we only have Nick's supposition that Gatsby had a capacity for tragic depth, we know it must have been so for Fitzgerald, for, surely, at least in the above passage, Fitzgerald is writing of his own disillusionment with the Roaring 20's, with the society of wealth that he frequented and, of course, with the American Dream. For Fitzgerald, then, "The tragedy that has become for so many one of the great revelations of what it has meant to be an American at all, was possible only because it was so profound a burst of self-understanding."[30] He realized, that is, the stark aloneness of the individual in America and the implied tragic implications of this situation.

III

It would seem plausible, then, to interpret *The Great Gatsby* as being supportive of the aforementioned Hobbesian-Lockean explication of the American sociopolitical consciousness. As in *The Scarlet Letter, Moby-Dick* and *Huckleberry Finn,* the hero is a highly individuated Self up against a social and cosmic order that is alien and hostile to him.

On another level, though, *Gatsby* can be perceived as not only supporting the above thesis, but also as indicating its further contemporary implications. It can, in other words, "be shown that

The Great Gatsby offers some of the severest and closest criticism of the American dream that our literature affords."[31] Individuated man in pursuit of happiness via the accumulation of wealth is the key ingredient of the modern American Dream, the inevitable mixture of Locke and industrialism — and it is this that *The Great Gatsby* not only describes but morally critiques. In *Gatsby*, fragmentation, the selfish, separate pursuit of alienated ends leads, as stated above, to "The Wasteland," to the ash-heaps, to loneliness, destruction, suffering and death. Thus, *Gatsby* goes beyond description to a normative evaluation of what it means to live in a contemporary Hobbesian-Lockean culture. Fitzgerald makes clear "the connection between Gatsby's individual tragedy and the tragedy of American civilization."[32]

This is exactly the case that Diggins proffers in *The Lost Soul of American Politics*, a book whose argument dovetails with all the novels discussed herein and, in particular, with Gatsby. Actually, on the surface, Diggins' book appears to be only a "full-scale assault on 'the republican synthesis,' especially as it has been formulated by the work of J. G. A. Pocock."[33] Diggins assails the civic republican theory as the foremost opponent of the liberal theory of American politics and tears it to shreds in a thorough and highly convincing defense of Hartz's *The Liberal Tradition in America*. But Diggins is after more than this. He is "angry with Pocock and the classical republican tradition only because they have prevented us from seeing ourselves as we really are."[34] He wants to "strip away the false classical coverings of our politics in order to reveal ourselves in all our naked liberalism. Diggins wants to assert Louis Hartz's thesis with a vengeance."[35] He "finds 'alienation' is everywhere in America" and "seems to delight in exposing the extent to which liberalism has created our 'fallen' alienated condition."[36] Like "a hellfire preacher" he argues that "only when we face our liberal reality honestly and admit our sins freely . . . will there be hope for us."[37] Like Fitzgerald, then, he wants to lay before us the reality of our liberal consciousness, served up in all of its strident, acerbic, individualist alienation. Cut off from each other, "isolates" through and through, we are, for Diggins, sinners all — locked in an individualistic ethic that is "bizarre,"[38] albeit monolithic, fundamental and all-pervasive.

Of course, it is one thing to realize you are in the Wasteland and quite another to get out of it. Neither Diggins nor Fitzgerald offers any really satisfactory escape from liberal fragmentation. Diggins offers a revitalization of Calvinist Christianity and an appreciation of the truly religiously motivated Lincolnesque hero[39] — but this clearly will not do. We are all, as participants in American culture, too steeped in modernity and postmodernity to return to theism or to expect our politicians to do so. As Wood states, "Perhaps it would be wonderful to believe once again in God and recover our lost soul. But there is no going back to those faithful days — at least not without a religious upheaval the like of which the Western world has not experienced in two thousand years."[40]

IV

But Fitzgerald does not have an easy solution for us either. In the end, he has Nick, really "the novel's central figure,"[41] although not its hero, go back home, back to the Midwest, back to that "vast obscurity beyond the city, where the dark fields of the republic rolled on under the night."[42] He has Nick return home to the values of a preindustrial America, to "a place of warmth and enduring stability."[43] But his return "is not a positive rediscovery of the well-springs of American life. Instead, it seems a melancholy retreat from the ruined promise of the East, from the empty present to the childhood memory of the past."[44] It is a retreat to the recollection of the restrained society of an earlier America when intermediary institutions were more effective in limiting the Self. But it is only nostalgia, like Twain's desire for the greater decency of a Jeffersonian America. After all, God has been reduced to the eyes of Dr. Eckleburg i.e. to just an advertisement. And the "bored, swollen towns beyond the Ohio, with their interminable inquisitions,"[45] with their attempted repression of the contemporary, expansive Self, as revealed in the work of Sinclair Lewis and Sherwood Anderson, offer obviously little serious comfort or effective, ego-limiting restraint in the end.

Returning home, then, is, for Fitzgerald, much what the desire for Calvinist Christian resurgence must be for Diggins — a moral impulse of longing, of hope, of vague aspiration, rather than any sort of affirmative, tangible alternative. In the last analysis, then, we can be made aware of our deepest sociopolitical problem, of our excessive individualism and innate lack of community, but doing much about it is not easy. If we are really Hobbesian-Lockean liberals to the core, then no real community is possible. Self-understanding is one thing, Fitzgerald can give us that, but redemption, Self-transcendence, is something quite different and it is as elusive as that "single green light, minute and far away"[46] that perpetually beckons to us. "So we beat on, boats against the current, born back ceaselessly"[47] into our liberal past.

But the elusive is not necessarily the impossible. The tragic vision, properly understood, is not permissive of real despair. Perhaps, then, driven by an ultimate extension of liberal autonomy, pressed to the existentialist parameters, we could begin to address the depth of individualist solitude and thereby limn the outline of an ontological commonality of purpose with others.

Notes

1. Irving Howe, *Politics and the Novel* (New York: Columbia University Press, 1957), 161.
2. Ibid., 162.
3. Ibid., 163.
4. Ibid., 200.
5. See Gordon S. Wood's review of Diggins' *The Lost Soul of American Politics* in "Hellfire Politics," *The New York Review of Books* 32, no. 3 (February 28, 1985): 29-32.
6. F. Scott Fitzgerald, *The Great Gatsby* (New York: Charles Scribner's Sons, 1925), 137.
7. Ibid., 40.
8. Ibid., 56.
9. Ibid., 21.
10. Ibid., 57.
11. Ibid., 58.
12. Ibid., 59.
13. Ibid., 50.
14. Ibid., 52.
15. Ibid., 37.
16. Ernest H. Lockridge, "Introduction," in *Twentieth Century Interpretation of The Great Gatsby* (Englewood Cliffs: Prentice-Hall, 1968), 5.
17. Fitzgerald, *The Great Gatsby*, 23.
18. Marius Bewley, "Scott Fitzgerald's Criticism of America," in *Twentieth Century Interpretation of The Great Gatsby*, ed. Lockridge, 44.
19. Fitzgerald, *The Great Gatsby*, 159-160.
20. Ibid., 158.
21. Ibid., 181.
22. Ibid., 23.
23. Ibid., 160.
24. Roger Lewis, "Money, Love and Aspiration in *The Great Gatsby*," in *New Essays on The Great Gatsby*, ed. Matthew J. Bruccoli (New York: Cambridge U. Press, 1985),46.
25. Fitzgerald, *The Great Gatsby*, 99.
26. William A. Fahey, *F. Scott Fitzgerald and The American Dream* (New York: Thomas Y. Crowell, 1973),70.
27. Fitzgerald, *The Great Gatsby,* 120.
28. Matthew J. Bruccoli, preface to *The Great Gatsby*, by F.Scott Fitzgerald (New York: Simon & Schuster, 1995), xi.
29. Ibid., 162.
30. Alfred Kazin, *On Native Grounds: A Study of American Prose Literature From 1890 to the Present* (Garden City, New York: Doubleday, 1942), 247.

31. Bewley, "Scott Fitzgerald's Criticism of America," 37.
32. Edwin Fussell, "Fitzgerald's Brave New World," in *The Great Gatsby: A Study,* ed. Frederick J. Hoffman (New York: Charles Scribner's Sons, 1962), 250.
33. Wood,"Hellfire Politics," 29.
34. Ibid., 30.
35. Ibid., 30-31.
36. Ibid., 31.
37. Ibid.
38. H. Mark Roelofs, *Ideology and Myth in American Politics* (Boston: Little, Brown, 1976), 252.
39. John Patrick Diggins, *The Lost Soul of American Politics: Virtus, Self-Interest and the Foundations of Liberalism* (New York: Basic Books, 1985),277-333.
40. Wood, "Hellfire Politics," 32.
41. Bruccoli, preface to *The Great Gatsby*, xii.
42. Fitzgerald, *The Great Gatsby*, 182.
43. Robert Ornstein, "Scott Fitzgerald's Fable of East and West," in *Twentieth Century Interpretation of The Great Gatsby*, ed. Lockridge, 59.
44. Ibid.
45. Fitzgerald, *The Great Gatsby*, 177.
46. Ibid., 22.
47. Ibid., 182.

Chapter 7

~~~
~~~

Literature, Individualism and Public Policy

I

Hawthorne, Melville, Twain and Fitzgerald were clearly all concerned with a powerful element of the American experience, a significant aspect of which troubled them. As supreme cultural analysts, they knew that individualism was the key to our deepest nature, that it was interwoven in the very fabric of what it meant to be an American.[1] Their perceptive artistic sensibilities led them to an intuitive comprehension of the American mind similar to Tocqueville's observational critique.

And, of course, it was Tocqueville who so clearly and perceptively, and, perhaps, best expressed the problem attendant upon the American love affair with individualism. In Book 2, Chapter 2 of *Democracy in America* he succinctly sums up the matter that the four novels essentially focus upon as well, Hawthorne's serpent within. Tocqueville states that:

> Egoism is a passionate and exaggerated love of self which leads a man to think of all things in terms of himself and to prefer himself to all.
>
> Individualism is a calm and considered feeling which disposes each citizen to isolate himself from the mass of his fellows and withdraw into the circle of family and friends; with this little society formed to his taste, he gladly leaves the greater society to look after itself.
>
> Egoism springs from a blind instinct; individualism is based on misguided judgment rather than depraved feeling. It is due more to inadequate understanding than to perversity of heart.
>
> Egoism sterilized the seed of every virtue; individualism at first only damns the spring of public virtues, but in the long run it attacks and destroys all the others too and finally merges in egoism.
>
> Egoism is a vice as old as the world. It is not peculiar to one form of society more than another.
>
> Individualism is of democratic origin and threatens to grow as conditions get more equal. . . .
>
> As social equality spreads there are more and more people who . . . have gained enough wealth and enough understanding to look after their own needs. Such folk owe no man anything and hardly expect anything from anybody. They form the habit of thinking for themselves in isolation and imagine that their whole destiny is in their own hands.
>
> Thus, not only does democracy make men forget their ancestors, but also clouds their view of their descendants and isolates them from their contemporaries. Each man is forever thrown back on himself alone, and there is danger that he may be shut up in the solitude of his own heart.[2]

Tocqueville's concern is clearly echoed in the four novels discussed in this text and from the above quote, one can appreciate his subtle understanding of the problem. Tocqueville initially distinguishes *individualism* from *egoism*, regarding the latter simply as selfishness and rooted in human nature. Individualism, on the other hand, develops as the result of the destruction of hierarchical sociopolitical order.

Initially a positive development, the valued repository of rights, individualism tends "to grow" and "merge in egoism," resulting in isolated selves "shut up in the solitude" of their own hearts. He proposes "associations,"[3] "self-interest properly understood"[4] and education[5] as modes of controlling and limiting the devolvement of individualism into pure egoism. Realizing, though, that in the future "Private interest will more than ever become the chief if not the only driving force behind all behavior,"[6] he foresees that Americans will have to make efforts to restrain their individualism for, if they do not, "it would be difficult to foresee any limit to the stupid excesses into which their selfishness might lead them, and no one could foretell into what shameful troubles they might plunge themselves for fear of sacrificing some of their own well-being for the prosperity of their fellow men."[7]

But individualism itself, according to Tocqueville, was indelibly written into the American soul. The only question was whether individualism, self-interest, could be *enlightened* or *restrained*. In the early 19th century, one could perhaps hope, as did Tocqueville, that strong civic association, religion and education could perform this function, but now, on the crest of the 21st century, it seems quite clear that they have not been able to do so. They have gradually faded under the unremitting pressure of a more and more unrestrained Self.[8] Nonetheless, Tocqueville's strategy of accepting the inevitability of individualism and then finding a mode of limiting it is still clearly the only reasonable way to approach the danger of excessive individualism.

My argument is that Hawthorne, Melville, Twain and Fitzgerald, when interpreted in the light of our postmodern experience, do indeed, by implication, offer support for Tocqueville's strategy for self-restraint. Given their perceptive insight into American culture, they were able to independently offer a creative, aesthetic response to American egoism which we can more properly appreciate for its highly contemporary elements. In the works that have been discussed, they, in effect, produce an analysis of the problem that parallels Tocqueville's. They also can be interpreted as offering a very modern, near existentialist suggestion as to what to do about it. Naturally, it is more helpful to regard their work in light of the American experience on the rim of the 21st century and this is the strategy employed here. We must understand them in terms of our own time.

II

If anything can be said with certitude about these four authors, it is surely that they are immersed in the ambiguity of American individualism. They perceive their heroes, and the larger American culture around them, at once positively and negatively. Hester Prynne, Ishmael, Ahab, Huckleberry Finn, Jay Gatsby and Nick Carraway, on the one hand, all have a heroic dimension. They often behave impressively and are usually the foci of interest. They are all highly autonomous persons, are all self-motivated and are of the most intense, deep character. They wrangle internally over their relations to others which are never easy. The Self-Other, individual-community problem is real to them and they struggle with it, some more directly than others. They are complex and self-reliant but always aware of their need for something beyond themselves. They realize or at least experience the inadequacy of their discrete particularity.

But the novels are also laced with evidence of a darker, egoistic individualism. The main characters often engage in excessively self-regarding behavior in one form or another and, of course, most of the people around them are primarily concerned with their own selfish purposes or aggrandizing enterprises. Twain fills the shores of the Mississippi with vulgar, stupid and rapacious selves. Ishmael's shipmates are mostly limited isolatoes, cabined in their own self-focused and non-reflective worlds. Hawthorne's Boston is largely peopled by believers in a simplistic, harshly repressive form of community and, of course, Gatsby's party people and the wealthy and underworld figures he associates with are routinely and appallingly greedy, selfish, duplicitous and shallow.

The main characters often disappoint as well. Huck's conduct, to say the least, is often far from exemplary. Gatsby foolishly believes that the unscrupulous acquisition of wealth will get him what he wants — Daisy's love. Ahab's excessive individualism turns him into a virtually isolated megalomaniac who believes he can do battle with God. Even Ishmael is at least partially drawn into Ahab's quest. Chillingworth's malicious self-centeredness nearly destroys Dimmesdale, but Hester's own early, opaque self-interest is ultimately responsible for the minister's downfall.

The main characters in the novels as well as, generally, the supporting casts, frequently display the very excessive individualism that tends to be the great problem at the heart of the American experience. The authors often critically portray "solutions" to this egoism that are clearly to be understood as, at best, inadequate and, quite likely, much worse than the problem they are trying to rectify. For example, Dimmesdale's self-repression, intended as a microcosmic version of general Puritan practice, is clearly unsatisfactory since it leads, in his case, to the ultimate destruction of his own self. Similarly, the Southern feudal world described in *Huckleberry Finn* is laced with its own lunacies. Subordination to family tradition or to codes of chivalry or to improper community values like slavery create worse problems. Also, Ahab's cosmological drivenness and his attempts to simplistically impose his will on those aboard the ship leads to the wreckage of the *Pequod* and, by implication, to the destruction of the society at large.

Ahab's Hobbesian tyranny, thus, is no answer to the excessive Self and his Self vs. All confrontation will not work. Similarly, Gatsby's materialist drivenness cannot overcome the Self-Other divide. Money cannot buy you love and lavish parties are not communities.

A clear message in these novels seems to be that community is never easily attained in the United States. One cannot simply take down from the shelf some standard answer to the Self-Other question and expect it to work. The Self is just too powerful in America. It is not going to be easily confined or rerouted. Regardless of whether the strategic response is religious (the Puritan world), political (Ahab's Hobbesian sovereignty), materialist (Gatsby's attempted connectives of wealth) or traditionalist (Southern feudalism), the Self is going to break through.

In the end, in all these novels, people are as alone as they were at the beginning of the tales and sometimes even *more* alone. The relief of community is not attained but the heroic characters do experience their aloneness, at the stories' conclusions, in a quite different manner. Given the Hobbesian rapaciousness and the pseudo alternatives all around them, Hester, Ishmael, Huck and Nick move in the only direction ultimately possible for them if they are to retain their integrity — they move within. They intensify their individualism by rejecting their negative environment and by determining to find their own way.

Huck heads off to the river. Hester embraces her isolation in Boston and Ishmael goes to sea because everyday living in America is becoming too much to take for him.[9] And Nick, in his "weatherbeaten cardboard bungalow,"[10] in the shadow of Gatsby's estate, but largely apart from the values of Gatsby's world, is nourished by a concern for moral behavior that is rooted in the social capital of an earlier America. If they must be individuals, then so be it, but they will act out their roles to the hilt. They will be autonomous Selves of substance, of real depth, as opposed to the superficial individuals around them.

The sense of apartness experienced by these key characters develops to what is, in effect, an existential situation. Whether fully conscious of the extent of their autonomy or not, Hester, Ishmael, Huck and Nick find themselves in circumstances that result in an experience of virtually cosmic isolation. Huck in his decision not to turn Jim in deliberately pits himself against God. Ishmael is very aware of his isolation on shore and on board the *Pequod*. It is he who refers to all on board as isolatoes, while his shipmates do not seem to fully appreciate their condition at all. At the novel's end, he is alone on the great ocean, floating on a coffin. Ahab, of course, makes God his enemy and immerses himself in his infinite isolation. Hester, after all that happens to her, winds up in a cabin on the outskirts of town, wholly alone. She offers advice to others but, in her own moments of need, can only resort to the sublime assuagement of tragedy for comfort. And Nick, cut off from his roots in the Midwest, is always separated by his moral decency from the world around him in New York, but no less alone and disconnected than everyone else.

The profound detachment experienced by these people is usually linked to their suffering. They are not happy in their self-generated removal from societal, from cosmic connectiveness. They agonize over choices they are compelled to make and wrestle with conflicting values. They struggle with the collision between what they believe to be right and what they are *supposed* to do, i.e. what society or God, what Other, demands of them. They deeply and personally experience the Self-Other, individual-community tension that is so wrapped into American sociopolitical reality and it causes them to experience deep inner turmoil.

Hester, for example, must contend internally with what she sees as the legitimate, contradictory demands of self and society. Huck must make the difficult choice between what society tells him about Jim, which he has always believed to be correct, and his personal experience of his friend. Ishmael must choose between what he is supposed to think about someone like Queequeg and, again, what he experiences himself.[11] He also fluctuates between participation in Ahab's mad quest and his own, sensible approach to Other. Nick must decide the extent to which he will become a part of Gatsby's (and Jordan's) world and the degree to which, for the sake of his integrity, he will remain removed from it.

With all of these people, the experience of isolation is deepened during the course of the novels. Hester, Huck, Ishmael and Nick must go through their journeys to fully develop their sense of disconnection, the trivial ending of *Huckleberry Finn* notwithstanding. Their stories are really self-inquiries during which they find out how really detached they are from the larger world around them. Ishmael, for example, philosophizes more extensively and darkly as the tale proceeds; Huck never thought, when he started his journey, that he would wind up standing up to God; Hester, only at the end, realizes how impossible her love for the minister was. Nick is forced to deal with issues he never imagined he would have to confront.

It is from their positions of anguished aloneness that these people reach out. Paradoxically, realizing the extent of their experiential severance from Other, realizing, more fully than ever before, that each person is really in a world enclosed, they come to experience that the root of their suffering is in this very detachment. Radically alone, they need to relate with Other, or *an* other, more than ever, but, equipped with an enhanced knowledge of the depth of their own solitude, they know this will not be easy and the goal, of course, is never realized. In the end, they are left with, perhaps, a sense of peace, of rest, that comes from a full realization of the great space that exists between one's self-consciousness and the reality of Other. Knowing the extent of this division, the nature of the gap, and knowing how difficult, if not impossible, it is to traverse it, but wanting, needing to do so, they experience a form of tranquility, a sense of having reached man's limits. They feel they know something about the nature of that space between Self and Other and that knowledge gives them a sense of participation in it, a sense of balance. After all, perhaps the best one can do in America, in terms of overcoming the Self-Other divide, is to know the nature of that division, to know how things really are, at least in terms of the depths of the American experience of metaphysical complexity.

Hence the great sense of rest at the end of *The Scarlet Letter*, *Moby-Dick* and *The Great Gatsby*. The key characters are not at one with anything at the conclusion of these stories, but they better see the nature of how things had always been and they therefore know something of composure, of comfort in the knowledge of man's fate.

Nick, for example, tells of how Gatsby's dream of oneness with Daisy, of overcoming completely the Self-Other division, of finding religious conclusion with her, "was already behind him" before

> he first picked out the green light at the end of Daisy's dock. . . . He did not know that it was . . . somewhere back in that vast obscurity beyond the city, where the dark fields of the republic rolled on under the night.
>
> Gatsby believed in the green light, the orgiastic future that year by year recedes from us. It eluded us then, but that's no matter — tomorrow we will run faster, stretch out our arms farther. . . . And one fine morning. . . .[12]

There is no real criticism of Gatsby here, but, instead, an acceptance, a wisdom of experience and insight on Nick's part that was wholly lacking in Gatsby and even in Nick, himself, earlier in the novel. Nick now discerns more clearly than ever that the American venture to achieve Self-Other union through materialism, to find God through Mammon, was doomed from the beginning. As he says, the first European colonizer, experiencing the sweep of the continent, must have held his breath and must have been "compelled into an aesthetic contemplation" provoked by being "face to face . . . *with something commensurate to his capacity for wonder.*"[13] (italics mine) Nick implies here that in America, from the beginning, it was always Self vs. Other, with each Self looking to the great continent as that which must be acquired, like Gatsby wanted to acquire Daisy. The project was invariably seen in essentially religious terms in that odd American blend of religion and materialism as, for example, was all of our talk about Manifest Destiny. The goal of oneness, of Self-Other community, could never be achieved, not in America certainly, with its acquisitive, rapacious, Hobbesian strategies for self-aggrandizing "success," but, of course, it cannot really be finally attained anywhere. Tragic wisdom indicates that the space between Self and Other is just too large, particularly if, as in America, the Self is virtually apotheosized. Fitzgerald and Twain and, more powerfully, Hawthorne and Melville, can tell us what Sophocles and Shakespeare knew.

In these four works, then, the Self-Other division is profoundly revealed in an American context and accepted. Many of the principal characters come to realize how difficult it is to connect with Other, but they all try — Ishmael reaches to Queequeg, Huck to Jim, Nick to

Gatsby and Gatsby to Daisy, Hester to Dimmesdale and, later, to the people in the village to whom she ministers. Even Ahab at least cares for Pip.

None of these struggling selves are happy alone. They do not want to be liberal *ens completa*, but, at their best, what they come to understand is that superficial, egocentric, bourgeois individualism leads only to the most inappreciable connectives with others. They come to understand that any real chance of community is only even remotely possible after the intensity of one's existential apartness is fully appreciated. Then it is all a matter of maintaining a Self-Other balance that has become more valid because of a newly deepened Self, a Self with an intense, virtually postmodern awareness that tries to approach equivalence with the profound, opaque facticity of Other.

Hawthorne, Melville, Twain and Fitzgerald, therefore, are paramount American writers because, in essence, they understand how profound our individualism is and further, they appreciate the necessity of the individual's coming to an awareness of this intensity. They know that, since we are a nation of isolatoes, community is, by that very fact, almost impossible to achieve. They know we can never abandon our liberalism, that it would not be in our nature, our cultural DNA, to do so, and that an expanding, depthless, merely bourgeois individualism will make a commonality of interest progressively more difficult. Only by acknowledging our expansive, imperial Selves and apprehending the full metaphysical dimension of our discrete singularity can we hope to realize the real importance and real possibility of relating to the non-Self, to the larger community.

III

In this sense, these writers are really proto-existentialist, accepting a radical aloneness, a radical liberalism, as the premise of valid self-awareness and the first step towards personal, and societal, responsibility. They anticipate later writers like Camus who will make much the same argument from within a more contemporary context.[14]

This is not to say, of course, that Hawthorne, Melville, Twain and Fitzgerald were really existentialist in any really formal sense, but rather that they implied a strategy of Self-Other relatedness in their work that shares common rooting with writers of our own time. Also, it should be recalled that European writers like Kierkegaard,

Nietzsche and Ortega y Gasset, recognized forerunners of existentialism proper, were part of a group that was essentially contemporaneous with the Hawthorne to Fitzgerald aggregate. As William Barrett argues, "By the middle of the 19th century . . . the problem of man had begun to dawn on certain minds in a new and radical form. Man, it was seen, is a stranger to himself and must discover, or rediscover who he is and what his meaning is."[15] So one could argue that these American writers constitute the same early modern perspective on the Self as do their coincident European colleagues, except that, in America, the analysis was made in particular acknowledgement of our extreme liberalism deriving from a uniquely American, Hobbesian-Lockean perspective.

Furthermore, the existentialist viewpoint itself is an outgrowth of a much larger continuum of Western thought traceable to the early roots of modernity and back further to ancient Greece.[16] This continuum is, in essence, the overall tradition of tragedy, the most profound and ancient of all perspectives. Certainly, this tragic outlook is clearly evident in *The Scarlet Letter* and *Moby-Dick* [17] and there are elements of it in *Huckleberry Finn* and *The Great Gatsby*.

In tragedy, the individual faces the great questions of life without the comforts provided by any particular interpretation of reality. All the "isms" and "ologies" are, at the end of the day, just stories that we tell ourselves in order to make sense of our existence.[18] Tragedy "recalls the original terror, harking back to a world that antedates the conceptions of philosophy, the consolations of the later religions and whatever constructions the human mind has devised to persuade itself that its universe is secure. It recalls the original un-reason, the terror of the irrational. It sees man as questioner, naked, unaccommodated, alone. . . . It is not for those who cannot live with unresolved questions or unresolved doubts." [19]

Ahab, alone against the universe, and Hester, struggling with unresolved contradictions and ambiguities, pit the Self against that obtuse reality that confronts anyone who wants to make sense of what life is supposed to be about. Of course, no one ever really knows the answer to this question, and great flawed characters like these two that press the limits too tangibly are roughly rebuffed. The fact that they quest so prodigiously, so mightily, generates our awe and respect, but there is also a disturbing drivenness about them that comes from believing too much in their own stories. Nick and Ishmael, more removed, more temperate, lack great passion but survive because they practice the ancient, classic values of composure and moderation. Hester does this too at the end and even Huck, a real survivor, is saved always by his balance and his reliance on an evened, common sense interpretation of experience. Tragedy, though, implies that the real issue of human existence, the disjunction between Self and Other generated by the very presence of our self-consciousness, is a permanent condition. We might go for long periods collectively persuading ourselves that this need not be so, but then there are times when

> the questions of ultimate justice and human destiny seem suddenly to have been jarred loose again. Often these critical periods, or "moments," come after a long period of relative stability, when a dominant myth or religious orthodoxy or philosophic view has provided a coherent and sustaining way of life. Suddenly the original terror looms close and old formulations cannot dispel it. The conflict between man and his destiny assumes once more the ultimate magnitude. It appears to be not a matter of accident, a temporary or limited disturbance, but an essential change in the face of the universe. The whole of society is involved, and the stake is survival.[20]

This tragic awareness was subscribed to by Hawthorne and Melville, who, by the mid-19th century, were at least intuitively cognizant of the fallacies of American liberalism. In effect, they no longer believed that a simple application of Lockean ideology to the Self-Other problem was going to work. They could see through the illusion; they could see that maximum autonomy, maximum *freedom from*, was going to leave us all alone, without community, and immersed in collision. So, for them, the primal question of how Self was ever to relate to Other was shaken loose again, as it had been for Shakespeare at the end of the Middle Ages and for the ancient Greeks at the dawn of the idea of individualism. Melville and Hawthorne had clear doubts about the American liberal culture and that disillusionment is evident in Twain and Fitzgerald as well. Self, they found, was, in America at least, intensely alone. This made the space between Self and Other virtually unbridgeable, leaving only the consolations of tragic composure.

But if their analysis of man in America was so stark, it did give them insight into tragedy and was the wellspring of their own greatness. They could not have probed any deeper nor cut a more discerning critique. We can infer that they held that if man was radically alone, then he must accept this without illusion and do his best to address the angst of this condition by attempting to relate to Other without deception. They knew that no final union with the non-Self would be possible and that neither self-abnegation (Dimmesdale) or hyperegotism (Ahab) would constitute a proper response to this situation. Only working that balance between Self and Other, a balance always new and always uniquely and creatively renegotiated, would give one the chance of the peace and composure that comes to those with tragic insight. Furthermore, in the age of democracy, in the age of the common man, the tragic vision would not be just for an Oedipus or a Lear but also for ordinary people like Hester, Ishmael, Nick and Huck, who reach deeply into themselves and stumble upon the profound.

The experiences, then, of Hester, Ishmael, Ahab, Huck, Nick and even Gatsby, in the awesome, sublime intensity of his passion, are the result of the existential concentration of the American Lockean liberal. With the particular exception of Gatsby, they have at least a moment in which they experience the cosmic depth of their autonomy. Even Huck, when he decides about Jim, is up against All. And Gatsby, while not self-aware, is yet driven by a virtually mythic passion that almost rivals Ahab's, a passion that presses him against the frame of his being and resonates with ontological depth. Huck, Ishmael *et al.* just do what they can, trying to remain true to themselves and struggling always to keep their balance. They are intense, but skeptical. They are radically self-aware and willing to accept the consequences. They see no easy answers but, above all, they want to keep the game going. They believe in life and in freedom and in the process of working that space between Self and Other even though this is done without hope of clear resolution. They are all survivors and sometimes, as in the case of Huck and Ishmael, they even possess a sense of humor. Life is good, they attest, even if we are cosmically alone. Self-conscious intensity will not save us, but it will keep us honorable and keep us from believing in false schemes of ultimate transcendence. Radically, intensely liberal, they find comfort in their enlightened autonomy and in their demystifying experiences.

But what they learn is that the individual must first come to terms with the fullness of his own autonomy. This deepens the need for Other and it makes community more desirable, if not more attainable. Community in America, then, is always really a wish, never a fulfillment. Thus, resolving the Self-Other division, perhaps metaphysically impossible anyway, is certainly not a facile proposition in a nation of extremely autonomous Selves, no matter how aware they might become of the liberal paradigm.

IV

What, then, are the suggestive implications for public policy that can be extrapolated from the analysis of the American mind supported and enhanced by these four authors? If their description of the metaphysics of the Self-Other relationship in America is accurate, and if a nation's public policy is based, ultimately, on its most fundamental understanding of itself in terms of how it responds to the essential Self-Other, sociopolitical question, then we should be able to garner some political insight from the above critique.

In this regard, the fact that the conception of autonomous individualism is entwined so deeply in the American character is clearly the foundation on which all else must be constructed. The immediate implication of this, of course, is that real community, one simply assumed and regarded as permanent, is rarely a part of the American landscape and present essentially as an exception to the rule. Instead, what generally passes for the experience of community is closer to an ad hoc, interest-oriented, superficial arrangement e.g. the self-help group, block association or protest organization. Such groups, including families and neighborhoods, tend to crumble under the unrelenting pressure of the ever expensive Self.

Individualism intensified in America, as was stated in Chapter 2, since it is the quintessentially ingrained American idea and, over time, over the past few centuries, the institutions that tended to obfuscate this reality withered and eroded. People have usually immigrated to America to escape the communities into which they were born abroad. They came in search of the individualism inscribed in our founding documents and in our generally successful economic system. They often brought with them anti-individualist religious and social ideas which they attempted to transplant, at least partially, in America but these ego-limiting cultural structures gradually faded or were reinterpreted in light of Hobbesian-Lockean individualism, leaving only the raw, egoistic Self. Thus, as the Self became less and less circumscribed and more unencumbered, whatever community existed in America tended to dissipate. By the end of the 20th century, the American individual, with the patina of community severely eroded, was more alone than ever.

Further, the stark American individual, given less and less reason for restraint, combined his/her negative freedom with the pursuit of materialist, capitalist success[21] to the general neglect of intellectual, artistic or relational purpose. So the unconstrained Self tends to interpret the absence of obligation as an opportunity for superficial aggrandizement.

In this context, government is perceived either as a vehicle to serve individuals qua individuals (welfare state policies including entitlement programs etc.) or it is perceived as a repressive structure limiting, virtually by its very presence, the individual's negative freedom. In other words, Americans dislike and distrust government except when it is doing something specifically for them. Government, then, in standard perception, is good when it does something for you and bad when it does something for the other guy. In either case, whether one wants to use government or minimalize it as much as possible, the end is the same. It is always a matter of government addressing and affecting the individual and never a matter of government being thought of as fostering community. Government always deals with the *Self* in America and not with the *Self-Other* relationship. There is often rhetorical talk about bringing people together, but this represents more a nagging Protestant conscience than a realistic program designed for actualization.

And there is no real turning back from this intensification of individualism. As the Self expands, fed by technological advancement and the decline of traditional institutions, wistful structures of community, never very deeply structured anyway, recede more and more. The process is relentless and proceeds in spite of a general bemoaning of the fact that this is happening.

With traditional institutions no longer retaining people's assumed loyalty, the only other structure strong enough to restrain the egoistic Self, government, is, of course, ruled out of consideration because of government phobia in America. Yet, intensifying individualism, resulting in more demands on government and less obligation to any real conception of community, leads to more societal deterioration. And government's inability to successfully address these escalating problems further undermines confidence in government and in the reality of the integrity of a commons, of a viable public sector.

The major political parties are not helpful in this context because they all speak the same language of individualism, only emphasizing different individualist agendas. The language of politics, then, the political imagination, is limited in America. All dialogue is essentially rooted in a capitalist, Protestant, materialist liberalism.

Meanwhile, problems persist due to the lack of any serious conjoined effort to thoroughly address public sector needs. Given the fragmentized nature of the American political system to begin with and the growing fear of and disenchantment with government, there is little wonder that so much of American life seems to be unsatisfactory. Whether one looks at crime, family dissolvement, a growing income disparity between rich and poor, a deteriorating infrastructure, illegitimacy, public and private debt, drug addiction, an under performing educational system, the decline of community values or numerous other concerns, the unremitting expansion of egoistic individualism has taken its toll.[22] And this general development, if not its particular manifestations, is what concerned Hawthorne, Melville, Twain and Fitzgerald, at least in an abstract sense, and what they intuitively projected as *the* problem of the American future. This is what they creatively warned us about.

V

It is possible, nonetheless, that a point has been reached where this expansive, acquisitive, yet shallow individualism is beginning to appear, at least in inchoate form, as a general problem of public awareness. There is a rising discontent in the American populace, a sense that something serious is wrong, that something has gone awry. There is a belief that our value system has deteriorated, that there is, in effect, too much individualism.

Of course, this discontent has been registered, in the electorate, as an attack on government, in which government is criticized for being too big, while, at the same time, repressive, Hobbesian measures are suggested in order to use government to restrain Selves that are obviously lacking self-restraint[23] The electorate blames first one political party and then another and flirts with the idea of a third major party. In classic American form, government is blamed for being too big and limiting the people's freedom while, at the same time, being unable to solve serious problems.

Given the extremely fragmentized nature of our political system, the fact that there are more than 80,000 essentially independent governing bodies in America,[24] it is not surprising that government is unable to deal effectively and thoroughly with any really major issues, particularly ones involving a lack of self-restrained behavior e.g. crime, drug abuse, family breakdown, educational deterioration etc. The problem, basically, is that Lockean government, on all levels, is essentially too weak, too divided, to do that which the Founding Fathers believed people would do for themselves in terms of restraining their own self-regarding conduct. It is, then, a frustration with weak government's structural inabilities to do that which people do not *really* want government to do i.e. restrict excessively individualistic behavior, that leads to feelings of powerlessness and expressions of voter anger.

In the end, though, people are not willing to blame themselves for their own culturally rooted excessive individualism, which is understandable given the noble, historical roots of our liberalism and the fact that it has only slowly, steadily, over centuries, become less restrained. This slow devolvement, at each level, thus gives the appearance of "normality." At each stage, the less circumscribed Self presumes that its level of freedom is appropriate. Of course, the same general fading of limits that one deems satisfactory for oneself is not realized to be the basic cause of the socially deviant or inappropriate behavior of the other. The problem is the general abandonment of self-restraint, a situation that neither government nor severely weakened intermediary social institutions can remedy since deference to the latter is no longer assumed and, additionally, being operant in a liberal context, they lack the degree of repressive force necessary to impose restraint on fiercely independent selves.

If the basic American cultural problem, then, is our extreme, substantially shallow but ever expansive, unrestrained individualism, if this is, indeed, our serpent within, then it is critical to develop a valid strategy to deal with it. This is not easy to do since we have become progressively unable to relate to the non-Self and to coherently address public sector problems. Politics devolves more and more into a strident collision of interests in which stronger interests prevail over weaker ones and the political process lapses into a continuous zero-sum confrontation.

But this road of expanding self-interest would not have to be a cul-de-sac. Whether it becomes one or not could depend one whether Americans could alter their interpretation of their ingrained individualism. What began with the Puritans, at Plymouth, as a morally and religiously circumscribed individualism, an individualism whose *purpose* was to achieve a generally metaphysical end, evolved into an individualism primarily oriented toward material attainment, towards pleasure, immediate experience and often factitious needs.

An alternative that could be elicited from the essentially conjoined critique of the four novelists addressed in this study would be to view our individualism again as a metaphysical situation. In other words, individualism would be accepted as it exists now, as an absolute in America, as the bedrock of the American mind. But then, instead of focusing on the Self's activities in the marketplace and within the popular culture, individualism would be taken to the nth degree, to its metaphysical roots. The individual would indeed perceive itself as a wholly autonomous entity, existentially positioned apart from Other and without the support of illusions. This would be a radicalized liberalism (from the Latin *radix* for root) because it would concentrate the independent Self and cast it not primarily against the other Selves in a quest for goods but, instead, against the entire cosmic non-Self, not to destroy the non-Self, but to deal with it as it is. One would emulate Ishmael, not Ahab. This would intensify the Self-Other division and raise it to a much higher level while, at the same time, de-emphasizing differences on the societal level. Hence, by making the Self *more* alone, existentially alone, the Self-Other division becomes cosmic, as was the case with Ahab, and societal conflict, while inevitable, is no longer the prime ground of Self-Other distinction. Other becomes *more* Other than ever, thereby profoundly intensifying individuality and leading the Self to realize that he/she must work the Self-Other division for much higher stakes than those available on the level of bourgeois societal interchange. As the Self-Other division is magnified, then, the *need* to overcome it is likewise magnified and the focus of one's energy is on matters that transcend "the petty pace from day to day" that so depressed Macbeth.[25]

Up against All, like Hester, Ishmael and Ahab, the radicalized Self, the existentially autonomous individual, will have intensified itself so that it is on a par with Other and focuses on how to relate to it, either through art, philosophy, religion, interpersonal relatedness or some other creative/intellectual/emotional methodology. As with the early liberals in America, then, attention is placed, at least ideally, on a larger, more profound plane of value which would then inform the ordinary level of liberal interchange and make the inevitable individual-community conflict on the latter stage appear to be less vital. Being regarded as less significant, then, this ordinary conflict would generate less heat and appear more resolvable since such collision essentially distracts one from the higher level of ontological tension which naturally ought to be one's main focus.

On this basis, a form of postmodern community can be developed, not by softening the edges of liberalism, as the communitarians argue, but by doing the reverse, by thoroughly intensifying it, for if the extent of one's autonomy is fully realized, one realizes how cosmically alone

one is and one also realizes that others must be in the same situation. As Camus argued, there is a kind of camaraderie in this awareness.[26] This is Lear's realization — and Ishmael's. Once shorn of illusions of purpose and meaning, the human tie of kindred isolatoes is clear. In this regard, recent studies of the quintessential postmodern Self, Samuel Beckett, suggest that, indeed, "He was a generous soul . . . who tried to relieve the suffering of others because he felt his own so deeply.[27] This is presumably what one would expect from someone who would adopt such a cosmically individualist stance.

By radicalizing liberalism, by going to the roots of the liberal idea, the stakes are seen as being so metaphysically high as to make ordinary matters of interest politics seem much less compelling. In fact, an emphasis could ostensibly be placed on finding solutions to conflicts of interest so as to prevent them from expanding and disrupting the higher level quest for Self-Other resolution. The overriding goal would be social peace which could only be achieved if Madisonian interest collisions were seen not as win-lose, zero-sum games but, instead, as disruptions of the social harmony requisite for necessary attention to metaphysical concerns. Competing liberal claims then become more like annoyances than like pit bull clashes in which all of one's primary efforts are focused.

Thus, realizing that all men/women are existentially isolated and struggling to find meaning in a Sisyphean enterprise focuses one's attention on where one's major efforts should be made and makes immediate problems much more resolvable. After all, people struggle over basically two things — either values or material goods. Since no one can finally be certain about the absolute nature of the former (although people usually act as if they are) and since material disputes are, by their nature, generally subject to compromise, in theory, human conflict, while inevitable, need not always be terminal or ultimately destructive. If, that is, the Hobbesian war of all against all must always exist, since we are such autonomous Selves and becoming more so, it need not be hopelessly bellicose in practice. By realizing a higher level of metaphysical importance and accepting its implications, a lid is placed on conflict not unlike the lid placed on conflict by Hobbes' sovereign. The difference, of course, is that the restraint on individual behavior is self-imposed by enlightened individuals, as was the case in the early days of the republic, rather than by an exterior political force, but the result is the same. Interpersonal disaccord is diminished so that that which gives nobility to human life, participation in the highest level of Self-Other encounter, is made possible. This is why Hobbes wanted the sovereign to have absolute power, so that the individual would be able to pursue ends higher than acquiring bread and staying alive. In the postmodern, more democratic world, the individual must be his own sovereign and impose restraint on herself/himself.

What this would do is reintroduce a metaphysical theme to liberal politics and go far towards addressing the key problem of excessive egoism portrayed by Melville, Hawthorne, Twain and Fitzgerald. Further, the nuanced distinction they generally made between types of individualism would be further developed in the above scenario. The world of commerce, negative freedom, immediate interest and material gratification would operate on a first tier of human interaction, but it would be conducted with the intention of establishing a foundation for the metaphysical, Self-Other interaction of a second tier.

Of course, metaphysically grounded self-restraint has existed in America before. In the early days of the American nation, much of the inevitable sociopolitical collision was less intense and egoism was more restrained because American society was informed by a Judeo-Christian consensus and a deference to authority that softened conflict on tier one. What was done on tier one was seen in the light of a theocratic tier two. So now the question is whether or not this type of restraint can be revived to any satisfactory degree again.

In this sense, Hawthorne, Melville, Twain and Fitzgerald realized the weakening of Judeo-Christian restraint more perceptively than most others. They saw an end to the old metaphysical answers and its inevitable subsequent effect on American life. They realized a need for something new and, particularly in the case of Hawthorne and Melville, offered essentially the consolations of the tragic tradition.

The two tier construct proffered here would essentially give a formal order to that tragic perspective. The lessons of tragedy, largely the wisdom of the few, of the aristocratic temperament, throughout Western history, would be experienced now as a more widespread observation. Oedipus and Lear and Hester came to regard the first tier world in a much different way after the depths of experience that they went through and, similarly, in a democratic age, there could come a point where there is a general societal acceptance of a tragic distinction between levels of importance. Such a widespread tragic awareness could do much to restrain the serpent of egoistic, Hobbesian-Lockean individualism and seriously affect public policy.

Melville, Hawthorne, Twain and Fitzgerald all realized that some people, at least, could come to distinguish the philosophically important from the non-important but they wrote long before our present age of generalized disappointment. The language of disillusionment is often standard currency now, even if a full understanding of the meaning of tragedy certainly is not. The key, then, is to transcend narrow affiliation to tend to the matters of the first tier while informed by the restraining presence of the second, thereby reducing rather than exacerbating the war of all against all.

In light of the above tragic perspective, what could this possibly mean in terms of practical politics? Leaving aside party affiliations and professed ideological differences, which matter little in the sense that virtually all of American politics has a common liberal base, there would be at least two general political concerns that could be speculatively envisaged.

First, government must vigorously protect the structure of rights that has been developed and expanded since the nation's founding. This would permit the continued individual autonomy necessary for the ultimate individualized development of a second tier, for tragic awareness and, hence, for a concomitant Self-limiting of first tier wants and desires. Having *government* restrict the Self would not work because (a) government is an extremely clumsy tool for doing this and (b) government is too limited and fragmented to accomplish this task effectively anyway. In other words, imposed self-restraint, besides being oxymoronic, cannot work to any ultimately effective degree because it completely contradicts the evolving, expansive, self-aggrandizing American individual consciousness. Ultimately, only the Self can effectively restrain the Self.

Second, there would have to be a general governmental consensus on maintaining not only a fully functional social "safety net," not just a minimal level of support for those in extreme need, but also a general agreement on maintaining the basic foundation necessary to achieve the possibility of a second tier consciousness. In other words, people should not have to spend all of their energy acquiring the minimal needs of modern life so that they are never able to arrive at a point where they are focusing on what it means to be human, on higher Maslovian concerns. For example, regardless of income, everyone should be entitled to the type of education that often only the wealthy can afford. Freedom from pressing want and access to accumulated, intellectual perspectives would help to provide the basis for the flowering of transcendent, self-restraining concerns that would be in the interest of all. Housing, health care, job training and assistance for the arts would be similar foundational supports. Such mainstays of a proper first tier existence are often begrudged those with fewer assets, those who have not been "winners" in the Hobbesian competitive struggle, because the "winners" cannot see how it is in their interest to provide for these others. But if the first tier "winners" understand their individualism not only in a Hobbesian-Lockean sense but also in an expanded existentialist/tragic sense, then it *does* become in their interest to support policies that would result in a generalized self-restraint which would make *their* existence in a highly individualized America more secure. Such policies would also give concrete, first tier expression to a balanced, second tier Self-Other relationship.

VI

In conclusion, then, *The Scarlet Letter, Moby-Dick, Huckleberry Finn* and *The Great Gatsby* can be interpreted in such a manner as to suggest a radicalizing, an intensifying of our inexpungable individualism. What can be derived from these works is something that is never didactically expressed, because these are works of art and not philosophical tracts. Instead, the nature of their argument is obliquely suggested, thereby providing provocative material for political theory. Read in this sense, an argument can be made that these books, amongst the most insightful American novels, offer an existentialist / tragic dimension to American Hobbesian-Lockean liberal political theory, not to replace it but to augment, control and transcend it. They offer a subtle, indirect but generally congruent critique that can be articulated in terms of political theory and that can even, by logical extension, be indicative of overall, but very broad, public policy directions.

Therefore, if Americans are to always be Melvillian isolatoes, and always to be threatened by the serpent within, there is nonetheless a transcending aspect to this condition that can add *gravitas*, self-control and even a type of human solidarity, if not community, to an inevitable existential reality of stark autonomy. And an enlightened politics can play a role in the development of this dimension.

If the "ripeness is all,"[28] according to Shakespeare, if the full unfolding of the individual, in all dimensions of its metaphysical maturity, is the most purposeful project, then, surely, Melville, Hawthorne, Twain and Fitzgerald have helped the American individualist mind to advance towards this expansion.

Notes

1. Seymour Martin Lipset argues that "the emphasis in the American value system, in the American Creed, has been on the individual." See Lipset, *American Exceptionalism: A Two-Edged Sword* (New York: W.W. Norton, 1996), 20.
2. Alexis de Tocqueville, *Democracy in America*, ed. J.P. Mayer (New York: Harper and Row, 1969), 506-508.
3. Ibid., especially chapters 4 and 5.
4. Ibid., chapter 8.
5. Ibid., 528.
6. Ibid., 527.
7. Ibid., 528.
8. See Robert D. Putnam, "Bowling Alone: America's Declining Social Capital," *Journal of Democracy* 6, no. 1 (Jan. 1995): 65-78.
9. Herman Melville, *Moby-Dick* (London, Collins, 1977),17.
10. F. Scott Fitzgerald, *The Great Gatsby* (New York: Charles Scribner's Sons, 1925),9.
11. Ishmael's intention in going to sea is to learn and experience, so he expects to challenge his preconceptions. This is what real learning is all about. He is, after all, really a teacher by trade. Hence, he appears to agonize less than the key characters in the other novels, perhaps because he expects disorienting situations to occur and is, in fact, looking for them. He goes to sea to experience change. Hester, Huck and Nick have their inner conflicts thrust upon them.
12. Fitzgerald, *The Great Gatsby*,159.
13. Ibid.
14. For an argument as to how Camus's work can be related to American individualism, see Joseph Bertolini, "Liberal Man in Cosmic Rebellion: Camus's Relevance to American Politics," *Michigan Academician* 28, no. 2 (March 1996): 97-112.
15. William Barrett, *Irrational Man* (Garden City, New York: Doubleday, 1962), 177.
16. See Walter Kaufmann, *From Shakespeare to Existentialism* (Garden City, New York: Doubleday, 1959).
17. See Richard B.Sewall, *The Vision of Tragedy* (New Haven: Yale, 1980).
18. Ernest Becker argues that all of these cultural value systems are really constructs designed to deny the reality of our finitude. See *Denial of Death* (New York: Macmillan, 1973).
19. Sewall, *The Vision of Tragedy*, 4-5.
20. Ibid., 7.
21. Richard Hofstadter, *The American Political Tradition* (New York: Random House, 1948),16.

22. For data on the societal cost of egoistic individualism see Lipset, *American Exceptionalism* and Urie Bronfenbrenner et al., *The State of Americans: This Generation and the Next* (New York: Free Press, 1996).
23. Legal curfews for young people, public school uniforms, increased use of the death penalty, longer jail sentences and the weakening of the exclusionary rule would be examples of proposed Hobbesian measures.
24. H. Mark Roelofs and Gerald L. Houseman, *The American Political System: Ideology and Myth* (New York: Macmillan, 1983).
25. Shakespeare, *Macbeth*, act 5, scene 5.
26. See Albert Camus, *The Rebel* (New York: Knopf, 1956).
27. Richard Corliss, "Dispelling the Gloom," *Time* 148, no. 10 (August 20, 1996): 57. See also, Mel Gussow, *Conversations With and About Beckett.* (New York: Grove, 1996); Lois Gordon, *The World of Samuel Beckett, 1906-1946* (New Haven: Yale, 1996); and James Knowlson, *Damned to Fame* (New York: Simon & Schuster, 1996).
28. Shakespeare, *King Lear*, act 5, scene 3.

Index

Abbot, Philip, 24, 25
acceptance, 35; of apartness, 37; tragic, 40, 41, *see also* tragic perspective
Adams, Henry, 9
alienation, 4, 58, 60; comprehension of, 60; in *Gatsby,* 80; from society, 67. *See also* isolation
American culture, 4–5; competing views in, 23–24; flaws in, 5; as Hobbesian-Lockean, 6, 8, 9, 19–20, 69; individual isolation in, 83–85, 96; individualism in, 2–5, 8–9, 65–66, 89; Lockean individualism and, 14, 66, 101; Lockean liberalism and, 13, 22, 84, 98; metaphysical assumptions of, 51; preservation of, 62; public policy and, 101–3
authors, American, 3; depiction of American culture by, 6; as proto-existentialists, 97–98; view of individualism, 4–5, 109. *See also individual authors' names*

Barrett, William, 98
Beckett, Samuel, 106
Bellow, Saul, 3, 66

Calvin, 18, 21
Camus, Albert, 97, 106
capitalism, 19, 20, 22, 73, 101
Christianity, 33, 84
Civil War, 32
Clemens, Samuel. *See* Twain, Mark
Coleman, Frank, 14
communitarianism, 22–23, 105
community: in America, 101; concept of, 3; connection with, 1, 43; negative, 43; possibility of, 85–86, 93, 96–97, 100, 105–6; sense of, 14

competition, 15
conflict, 14–15, 32, 106
Conrad, Joseph, 9
conservativism, 45; religious, 20
Coxe, Arthur Cleveland, 32
cruelty, 69–70
culture, American. *See* American culture

defiance, 53–54
dictatorship, 16, 17
Diggins, John Patrick, 24, 84
Dostoevsky, Fyodor, 9

egotism, 2, 74, 90, 107; consequences of, 37. *See also* individualism; self
"Egotism, or the Bosom Serpent," 1
Eliot, T.S., 80
evil, 16; excessive individualism and, 41, 43
existentialism, 97–98
experience: conflict between society and, 94–95; nature of, 59–60, 71

facts, 71
family, 19
Faulkner, William, 3
feudalism, 14
First World War, 5
Fitzgerald, F. Scott, 3; as cultural analyst, 4, 89, 91; *The Great Gatsby,* 5, 79–86; incorporation of cultural perspective, 8; tragedy and, 83, 84, 99

good, 16
government: as enemy, 16, 18, 103; limitation of, 18, 20; Lockean, 20, 25, 103–4; purpose of, 15–17, 20, 102; roles of, 22, 102, 108–9

The Great Gatsby, 5, 79–86; materialism in, 82; negative individualism in, 80
Gross, Seymour, 34
groups, 21–22
guilt, 23, 37, 65

Hartz, Louis, 8, 9, 13, 25; critiques of, 24, 84; on Lockean liberalism, 68
Hawthorne, Nathaniel, 1, 2, 3; as cultural analyst, 4, 89, 91; darkness of writing, 32–33; incorporation of cultural perspective, 8; isolation and, 36–37; *The Scarlet Letter*, 31–45; tragic awareness and, 99
Hemingway, Ernest, 3, 72
Hobbes, Thomas, 14; on government, 17, 107; on human nature, 14–15, 26; on Other, 52
Hofstadter, Richard, 14, 25
Howe, Irving, 9, 79–80
Huckleberry Finn, 65–76; connection of individuals, 67–68, 75; Huck as rebel, 66, 68–69; as nonpolitical novel, 9; presentation of Hobbesian-Lockean individualism, 75
Hume, David, 52
Hutchinson, Anne, 38, 44

individual: in American literature, 65–66; autonomous, 67, 71, 105; as center of meaning, 53, 55, 57, 74; growth of, 45, 108–9; importance of, 20–21; as law, 38–39; Lockean, 68; self-interest and, 16; self-restraint and, 25–26, 101, 106–7; social restraint of, *see* institutions, intermediate. *See also* self
individualism, 1; ambiguity of, 92; American, 34, 55; American culture and, 2–5, 8–9, 65–66, 89; American expansion of, 18–21, 24, 91, 104; complexity of, 19; consequences of, 3, 26, 35, 36–37, 83–84, 103; destructive, 84, 90; excessive, 55, 91, 92–93, 103; as evil, 41, 43; forms of, 4, 5, 107; groups and, 21–22; Hobbesian elements in, 18–20, 65, 68, 75; intensification of, 66, 82, 86, 93–94, 101, 104–8; liberal, 20; materialistic, 5; metaphysical supports for, 33, 104–6; Puritan, 5, 21, 38, 104; religion and, 19, 20, 21, 23, 25; responses to, 10, 93, 99–100, 102–3, 104–9; self-referential, 5; separation of religion from, 33–34; social deterioration and, 101–3; Tocqueville on, 19, 90; unconstrained, 14, 18–19, 91. *See also* egotism; self
institutions, intermediate, 14, 17, 18, 23, 25–26, 85; failure to restrain individualism, 91, 101, 104
introspection, 68, 70–72, 76. *See also* self-knowledge
Irving, John, 3
isolation, 2, 67; awareness of, 34, 41, 44–45, 60, 61, 80, 83, 94–95, 97; as commonality, 61, 105–6; destruction by, 41–43; literary depiction of, 80; as opportunity, 70; relief of, 31; self-awareness and, 97, *see also* introspection; transcendence of, 32, 41, 85

James, Henry, 3

Kant, Immanuel, 52, 61
Kierkegaard, Soren, 97
Klein, Joe, 9
Kymlicka, Will, 23

liberal culture, Hobbesian-Lockean. *See* American culture
liberalism, 13, 18; alternatives to, 85; American, 21–23, 51, 55, 84, 97; community and, 100; fragmentation by, 84; guilt and, 23, 65; Hobbes and, 16; intensification of, 61; minorities in, 24; radicalized, 105–6; types of, 22, 24, 66. *See also* politics
literature: ideological foundation of, 6; political novels, 9; as tool of comprehension, 6–7, 8, 35, 51, 65, 109
Locke, John, 61; basic philosophy, 13–14; on government, 16; on Other, 52
loneliness, 67, 80
love, 44

Macpherson, C. B., 14, 24
materialism, 5, 82, 93, 96, 101
media, 26
Melville, Herman, 3; as cultural analyst, 4, 89, 91; on Hawthorne's work, 32; incorporation of cultural perspective, 8; *Moby-Dick,* 51–62; tragic awareness and, 99
metaphysics: American cultural assumptions, 51; individualism and, 33, 104–6; ultimate answers in, 57
misperception, 44, 59
misunderstanding, 32
Moby-Dick, 33, 51–62; Ahab's view of Other as evil, 53–55; extreme individualism as madness, 55; Self-Other balance in, 56–60
More, Paul Elmer, 33, 34

nature, state of, 14, 15–16; in *Huckleberry Finn,* 68
New Deal, 22

Nietzsche, Friedrich, 98
novels, political, 9

obligations, 21, 40, 102
Ortega y Gasset, José, 98
Orwell, George, 9
other: as autonomous self, 72, 75, 105; balance with Self, 43–44, 45, 56, 62, 66, 95, 99–100; destruction of Self by, 52, 53, 54–55, 93; division from Self, 95–96, 99, 105; failure of connection to Self, 35; individual's quest re, 53–55, 60; knowledge of, 52, 55–57, 59–61; need for, 75; as obstacle, 15; relation to Self, 4, 24, 55–60, 67, 96–97, 105–6; use of, 52. *See also* individualism; self

Pocock, J. G. A., 24, 84
political philosophy, 7–8
politics: foundation of American, 17–18, 24, 102; ideological foundation of, 6; in literature, 79–80; nonliberal, 21, 23; in personal experience, 79; radicalized liberalism and, 108–9; use of literature to understand, 6–7, 8, 35, 51, 65, 109. *See also* liberalism
primitivism, 70
Puritans, individualism and, 5, 21, 38, 104

radicalism, 14
religion, 107; in *The Great Gatsby,* 81–82; in *Huckleberry Finn,* 70–71; individualism and, 19, 20, 21, 23, 25, 33–34
resignation, 35
responsibility 3, 21, 97; general social, 40
rights, 3
rivalry, 15
Roelofs, H. Mark, 14, 19, 24, 25

Index

Salinger, J.D., 3
salvation, 59-62, 70, 75, 85
The Scarlet Letter, 31-45; critiques of, 35; depiction of isolation, 31, 33; Hester as individualist, 38-40; portrayal of excessive individualism, 41-44; sin in, 44; tragic dimension of, 34-35
self, 3; autonomous, 13, 14, 16; balance with Other, 43-44, 45, 56, 62, 66, 95, 99-100; division from Other, 95-96, 99, 105; evil of, 42; extinction of, 52-53, 55; failure of connection to Other, 35, 43, 44-45; God and, 69; isolated, 36, 61; need for Other, 75, 95; relationship to Other, 24, 55-60, 67, 96-97, 105-6; repression of, 41-42, 45, 85, 93; tragedy and, 34-35, 52; transcendence of, 37, 75, 85-86. *See also* community; individual; individualism; other
self-concern. *See* egotism; self-interest
self-inquiry, 70
self-interest: constraints on, 14, 17, 104; enlightened, 73; as motivation, 16
selfishness, 19, 42, 69; in *Gatsby,* 84
self-knowledge, 41. *See also* introspection
self-realization, 71
self-restraint, 42, 91; abandonment of, 104; imposed, 108; individual and, 25-26, 101, 106-7
sin, 44
Smith, Adam, 18

Smith, Rogers M., 24
social interrelationships as constraint on self-interest, 14, 17, 18
society, bonding in, 80. *See also* community
Solzhenitsyn, Aleksandr, 9
Strauss, Leo, 14
Styron, William, 3
suffering, 35, 40, 94

theism, 85
Tocqueville, Alexis de, 8, 19, 89-90
tragedy, 44, 94, 98-99; destruction of self, 52
tragic perspective, 34-35, 45, 66, 98, 107-8; Fitzgerald and, 83
transcendentalism, 33, 34
Twain, Mark, 3; as cultural analyst, 4, 89, 91; *Huckleberry Finn,* 65-76; incorporation of cultural perspective, 8; tragic awareness and, 99; view of human nature, 69-70, 74, 76; view of liberal individualism, 73-74; view of socialization, 74

understanding, 57, 82-83
Updike, John, 3

values, priority of, 81, 106

"The Wasteland," 80
"Wakefield," 36-37
wealth, 5
Whitman, Walt, 67
Wood, Gordon S., 85

HIEBERT LIBRARY

3 6877 00164 0795

DATE DUE

OC 06 '03			
NO 03 '03			

Demco, Inc. 38-293